UNVEILED

Fanny Chamberlain Reincarnated

JESSICA JEWETT

INTRODUCTION BY
JEFFREY KEENE

Madison,
    My hope is you find something in these pages to enhance your own sense of spirituality.

Love,
Jessica Jewett

For the believers.

ACKNOWLEDGEMENTS

A book about self-exploration of this enormity could certainly not happen without the support and guidance of a multitude of people behind the scenes. Throughout my life and my initiation into my work with reincarnation research, there have been people behind me nudging and encouraging me to reach my full potential, albeit with me occasionally kicking and screaming along the way.

First and foremost, I must take the opportunity to thank my family for their endless devotion to my happiness, mental and spiritual development. It cannot be easy to raise a child with such involved physical special needs but my family did so without complaint, pity or wallowing in what could have been viewed as a tragic misfortune. In each of their own ways, they instilled the tools and equipped me with the intelligence and ability to become my own person while questioning the world around me through independent thought.

I wish to thank my mother, Lori Graham, for teaching me to stand by my convictions no matter who tries to silence me. "If you don't learn to open your mouth and speak up for yourself," she told me when I was twelve-years-old, "people will walk all over you for the rest of your life." I not only speak up for myself now but for all of those who have felt suppressed in unorthodox beliefs for the sake of society's interpretation of normality.

Next, my gratitude goes to my uncle, Ben Jewett, who continually stepped into the shoes of surrogate father in my life when my own no longer wanted to fulfill that role. He and my grandmother, Lois Jewett, both taught me that there are some people who are capable of skepticism, belief and intelligent debate in paranormal matters without judgment or malicious intent. Their unconditional love pulled me through so many dark hours of self-doubt and self-loathing.

I also want to thank my brother, Michael Jewett, and his wife, Jessica, for their support before and through the process of writing this book. I am endlessly grateful for the second journey to Maine in which we visited the Chamberlain house and poured over document after document at Bowdoin College, searching for more clues about Fanny, Lawrence, Tom and Delia.

There were a great many friends who, through the process of investigating my past life of Fanny Chamberlain, became nothing short of family to me. Without the assistance of Beth Miller and her family, I would not have been able to make my journeys to Brunswick and Portland, Maine. Beth's assistance in editing this book, along with Nellie Kampmann, was invaluable.

Credit for assisting me in historical and spiritual research and photography in Maine over the years goes to: Janine DePuma, Lori Graham, Tracy Grondin, Michael and Jessica Jewett, Nellie Kampmann, Paul Karabin, Jeffrey Keene, Ciara Lee, Tom McDonald, Beth Miller, Kenneth Robinson II, Sarra Rohr, Kevin Ryerson, Dr. Walter Semkiw, Janet Smith and Dawn Solomon.

Many thanks go to the Maine Historical Society, the Pejepscot Historical Society, the Chamberlain Museum, and the Special Collections Department of Bowdoin College, each for their assistance with historical research into the Adams and Chamberlain families.

Lastly, I am inclined to acknowledge the truth that my life as Fanny Chamberlain might never have made such an impression upon my soul had Joshua Lawrence Chamberlain not been part of it. In this book, I discuss at length how love, like the soul, is deathless and when you share real, earnest devotion with another person, it can never die. He was a potent, compelling personality and his influence on me transcended time. One of my endeavors with this book is to use his most comfortable medium – the written word – to tell our story in a way that has never been told and to inspire hope that family, love and soul connections continue much longer than one lifetime.

INTRODUCTION
BY JEFFREY KEENE

We are all on a journey but seldom in our travels do we stop to travel inward. Sure, the world around us is filled with interesting sights; and often concerns for work and our social lives distract us. There is also another reason too few of us do some healthy introspection and that reason is fear. It takes courage to evaluate oneself, to be honest and open to all the realities that lay hidden just beneath the surface of our skin. The young lady who authored the story you are about to read has shown real courage, more so than most of the military people she writes about. Self-examination is one thing, but putting it out to the public takes things to a whole new level. Jessica's world is quite confining physically, but I have never met anyone with a freer mind. That mind has allowed her to study the world very deeply both inside and out. She may give credit for many of her insights to others but we all travel certain paths alone and decide whether to proceed or turn back. She has taken each step forward on her own and with eyes wide open. Many people can not conceive of the types of feelings and emotions Jessica talks about; for the only way to fully understand them is for one to have their very own personal contact with those experiences. Until you are ready to have your own adventure, let Jessica light the path ahead a little for you.

CHAPTER ONE

I wanted to die.

The decision was an easy one when faced with another year of pain, sickness, pills and doctors who appeared as clueless as I was about the cause of my illness.

That night in the spring of 2003, I lay in the quiet of my bedroom just outside of St. Louis feeling the pain and nausea radiate through my body. My doctors had decided that previous winter that it was an unspecified chronic kidney infection, yet having a name for the condition did little to inspire a cure for it. I became a student of suffering and I learned by experience that constant pain exhausts the body and soul quicker than anything else. I had been denied the comfort of sleep for months, save a few hours each night when I was not vomiting what little food I had managed to eat during the day. My life had gone on like this for five months by that night, an endless procession of late-night emergency room visits, catheters, intravenous lines, clueless doctors, pills and general misery with no resolution.

This is no way to live.

I remember that thought hitting me with such blinding clarity that I was dumbstruck by it for a long suspended moment.

This is no way to live.

Awed, I listened to the muffled sound of my brother's fingers clicking the keys of a computer keyboard in the living room, a strange sound of comfort simply knowing he was there. Michael sat up faithfully more nights than I could count, awaiting the inevitable fever checks, refilled water jugs and emptied catheter bags. My brother was only nineteen at that time and had silently given up any hope of going to college or finding meaningful work because his invalid sister could not be left home alone more than a few hours at a time. No one could have asked for a more dedicated brother and the guilt wore on my nerves. There was no one else to care for me in Missouri. I was holding my brother's young life hostage.

This is no way for either of us to live.

I began to wonder what it would feel like if I simply let go. Let go of life, let go of pain and let go of the feeling I had carried around in my consciousness for my entire life – I was a freak. Since I was a child, thoughts, feelings and memories of different people in different centuries had periodically forced their way to the surface of my thoughts, and the few times I confided in people close to me, I was met with denial and strange looks as if I was somehow mentally unstable or unabashedly weird. I fought hard to keep these things to myself. Being so sick every day for months left me with no energy to even acknowledge that I was experiencing spontaneous past life memories since I was a toddler. I knew what plagued my mind and soul by that night but the infection raging in my body prevented me from having the capacity to deal with it.

Indeed, how easy it would be to let go of my life and place my soul in the hands of God. That's exactly what I had been taught my entire life. God was all-forgiving an all-knowing. God would welcome me into the eternal kingdom of Heaven if I offered myself to Him. I would not be with my family anymore but at least I would not feel pain or sickness anymore either. A brief thought crossed my mind about my brother coming in to the room at 4 a.m. to check my catheter bag and finding me dead. Despite feeling pity for him, I only felt relief for myself and I knew he would understand someday, perhaps when an old man at the twilight of his own life.

I closed my eyes and felt the wind of breath pass through my body.

"Lord," I whispered to the ceiling above me, "I'm ready. I'm choosing my own time to go and this is the time. I'm placing myself in Your hands. I'm too tired. I can't do this anymore."

I waited. Somewhere in the back of my mind, I actually believed quite arrogantly that a person could bargain with the higher power. I had no idea what would happen. Would God come down from Heaven like a blinding white light? Would He come down from Heaven as a man? Or would He ignore me altogether? A person in their darkest hour of desperation cannot fathom being ignored by the one force who is supposed to love you unconditionally. I could not fathom God ignoring my pleas for help.

A voice broke my thoughts, though I'm not sure how much time had passed after I made the plea.

"Fan," the voice said.

My eyes popped open because the voice was so quiet that I wasn't certain I had heard it at all. I held my breath and debated about whether I had imagined it, if it was the wind blowing tree branches against my window outside, or if I actually heard a voice. I chuckled to myself, thinking what sort of a strange word the Almighty would pick to utter in my presence. Fan? Was God uncomfortable in my stuffy little room? Did He want me to turn on the fan? How typical of my luck, I thought, that I would make an honest desperate outreach from my heart only to be met with the universal life force asking me to turn on a fan instead of actually helping me.

Quite annoyed with myself, I sighed and quipped, "If You are going to take me home, Lord, then take me. I'm tired of waiting. I'm tired of being in pain. I'm tired of not being able to eat or think straight."

When I didn't receive another answer, I admit I was quite angry with God. I rolled over to face the wall with a huff and I prepared myself for another day of pills and catheter bags. I was too angry to sleep but I had gotten quite accustomed to functioning on no rest over that year.

"Fight, Fan. You have work to do."

Hearing the clarity of those words made my heart almost bolt straight out of my chest. My eyes darted around the room, searching in the dark for the person who spoke, but soon I realized I could not decipher with any certainty if the words came from the room or inside of my own thoughts. One thing was certain, however, and that was how familiar the voice sounded. I squinted in the darkness and found nobody else present in the room. The familiarity felt distant, like a finger reaching through the veil of a dream to touch me. Heaviness fell over the room that felt like trying to pull oneself through a dense body of water. Static charged the air, making my skin prickle like a limb regaining circulation.

No, I can't deal with that now, I thought to myself. I knew the owner of that voice telling me – "Fan" – that I had work to do. I knew him in my dreams since I was a toddler long before I knew his name or that he was a real man. I knew how the baritone of that voice resonated through a person when he sang in the nineteenth century. I also knew I had been suppressing the piece of me that he spoke to since I came across her identity in a Georgia bookstore in 1999. Denying her, that part of myself, I realized as I heard him tell me to fight my illness again and again in my thoughts, was no different than denying that he ever existed. It was no different than denying all the peaks and valleys of struggle we went through to be together, to have our family and our life.

"Lawrence?" I sent out the whisper into the darkness.

Of course I didn't receive a reply the rest of the night, but his words came through me with the force of a bullet. I had work to do. It was selfish of me to want to die and take the easy way out of this life, because a soul never has an easy way out. That night, at that exact moment, I had all the proof I needed and I accepted who I was, a person whose purpose in this life is to help others cope with theirs.

After that May night in 2003, I could say it and feel it deep in my soul.

I once was Fanny Chamberlain.

My work had begun.

CHAPTER TWO

A baby does not enter the world with any conscious knowledge of the concept of reincarnation. In most cases, parents have no reason to expose their children to things that might frighten them, but still, many children exhibit the uncanny natural ability to know things of the unseen world. Natural awareness of the journey of their souls through a variety of lifetimes is often, in Western society, shown to be a weakness or something of which to be ashamed or dismiss as nothing but make believe. A few children grow up unable to deny the truth of their past lives despite the pressures of society to bear what they view as the cross in silence. Truth, no matter how painful or shocking, rises to the surface whether it is welcome or not.

As a little girl, my intention was never to be a voice for people coping with the judgment inflicted by those who deny the existence of anything they could not touch in the tangible world. I never knew what the word "reincarnation" even meant until I was well into my teenage years. I only wanted to play with my Barbie dolls, Play-Doh and learn to read and write, yet the images, voices and feelings of a completely different life existed in the deepest parts of my mind. I endured the pressure by society to deny the very history of my soul and to be "normal" like everyone else for years but I came out of it with the realization that what is "normal" to me makes up the fabric of my existence. The awareness of my past life as Fanny Chamberlain, as with the life before that in revolutionary France, and the others reaching back hundreds of years, pushed into my conscious mind whether I wanted it or not. The more I fought it, the more the universe seemed to push me, to tell me that the understanding of the present cannot be completed without an understanding of the past.

Living this itinerant life in places all over the country with no real permanent home is a far cry from the decades Fanny spent building a home in a small college town on the coast of Maine. Perhaps it was the strong ties to home and family I had at that time and lacked this time that stirred memories of that life in my subconscious, pushing the images to the forefront of my mind. Perhaps it was nothing I did or saw that triggered my memories but a larger force choosing me to guide and inspire faith in others. I doubt I will ever truly know why this happened to me.

The phenomena of spontaneous past life memories exist whether it is believed or not. Just as certain things trigger memories into a few years past, or remind people of things in childhood, so too do people experience triggers for remembering events in previous lives. The unfettered mind of a child has the natural ability to recall such things but the training of society teaches the child to suppress these memories and forget completely. I could not forget. Even the battle to be normal against being myself brought on periodic bouts of depression and anxiety. Only when self-acceptance is achieved can people truly learn the unexpected joy and freedom that comes with independent thought and pursuit of one's own truth.

Fanny Chamberlain was born into the Adams family in Jamaica Plain, Massachusetts, on August 12, 1825. Her birth was unexpected since both of her parents were elderly at the time. She was a distant cousin to President John Adams but lived her earliest years in poverty among siblings that were about a decade older than she. The poverty forced her parents to give her up for adoption. After being passed around to different family members, she was finally surrendered to her father's childless nephew, Reverend George Adams, when she was merely four-years-old. She was brought up with a liberal education in literature, music, art and everything she would need, short of going to college.

After a lengthy courtship, she married Joshua Lawrence Chamberlain, who was born on September 8, 1828, on a farm in Brewer, Maine. They lived together in Brunswick, Maine, and had five children, although only two survived beyond infancy. He was a professor at Bowdoin College who effectively ended his academic career to fight for the Union in the Civil War. Remarkable leadership in the famed bayonet charge at Little Round Top and his near fatal wounding in the Siege of Petersburg led to promotions toward Brevet Major General at the end of the war and election to Governor of Maine for four terms after the war.

In the spring of 1984, I had no concept of the names Chamberlain, Adams, Fanny or Lawrence, as he liked to be called, nor did I have the dimmest conception of where to find Massachusetts or Maine. At that time, I was a two-year-old child dealing with the prospect of having to share my mother with a baby brother, Michael. It was something of a relief to the family that Michael was not born with my condition even though nobody ever treated me as "the special child." I was born in Denver, Colorado, with Arthrogryposis Multiplex Congenita (AMC), a congenital disorder marked by generalized stiffness of the joints, often accompanied by muscle and nerve degeneration, resulting in severely impaired mobility of the limbs.[1] That simply means my joints are fused, I have little muscle mass and the condition has left me a quadriplegic. Since my mother raised me with the philosophy that I am no different than anybody else, I rarely consider my condition in everyday life.

Most of my earliest memories were filled with heightened senses and the ability to think at a more advanced pace than other children. As with a blind person or a deaf person, when one natural ability is suppressed, the other senses work overtime to make up for the loss. In my case, I feel that my disability allowed me to be still and quiet enough to find the natural ability of spiritual intuition. There has never been a time in my life that I don't remember relying on what my intuition told me about people or situations. I never understood that the level of intuition I exhibited was not typical until I reached school age.

I was a creative child. Before I could even write a letter in the alphabet, I had the desperate, overwhelming urge to create, to

---

[1] *The American Heritage® Stedman's Medical Dictionary*

be artistic. My artistry ranged from drawing, to painting, to singing for hours and hours with my grandmother's record player. Early in my life, the things that stuck out in my memory the most were art, music and the dreams about people from another century. The dreams began so early and had such an impact on me that in times when I can recall every detail about one of those dreams, I cannot begin to describe what was happening with my family.

My first brush with an awareness of reincarnation came at this young age. I remember waking up from a nap in a large bed after sunset and I had forgotten where and who I was. The strangest sense of suspension of time and no longer experiencing time as a linear phenomenon overtook me. The past, present and future existed all at once in me, until my logical mind regained itself. It felt like an hour but it must have only been a few minutes as I lay on my back looking up at the ceiling with thoughts filling my head from what felt like a very adult part of me.

"Where am I? Oh, yeah. New family. Starting over again. I wish I could talk more."

Those were not typical thoughts for a two-year-old and, looking back on it, I see that my thought processes were never those of a child just beginning to develop language skills. I was always very aware of things unfolding around me despite not being able to articulate my feelings well enough. I describe it as clear, concise opinions formed in my brain being fed through a series of filters before they came out of my mouth in toddler's gibberish. My family still talks about how frustrated I could become when I could not get my feelings on any matter out adequately.

A few weeks later, my mother put me into the home of a new babysitter with my little brother. Most of my life at that time was lived on the floor because I was not able to pull myself up on furniture for a different perspective on things. I do not remember anything about the babysitter now, other than she was a rather large woman and I always rolled out of the way when she passed by because I was afraid of her falling on me.

A lot of people came and went out of that house. I still did not understand that I was different in any way, whether it was my quadriplegia or the occasional glimpse of translucent people that nobody else seemed to notice. I do remember some people looking at me with suspicion a few times in my life when I spoke to those translucent figures. To me, there was nothing unnatural about it. Children are simply not born with the inherent knowledge imposed by society that talking to "invisible" people or having memories of past lives are not what is considered normal. I had no idea that I was considered what they now term a child medium. The people in my life back then simply thought I was strange because I appeared to talk to myself.

There were other children at the babysitter's home as well. After we ate lunch one cloudy afternoon, the babysitter gated all of the children in the living room so she could watch her soap operas. One little girl in particular was about my age with thick dark hair cut into a blunt shape around her face. I remember wondering to myself if she knew that I had the same color hair as her "before."

That was the way of my childhood.

This or that was not how I lived "before."

I was too shy as a child to really talk to anyone in depth but people would never distinguish that about me now. As a child, I lived with an unexplainable instinctive fear that I should keep myself guarded and never show people too much of who I was or what went on in my mind. A secretive child, perhaps, and I have been that way as long as I can remember. There were a lot of children in that woman's home daycare but I never made friends with any of them. Instead, I kept to myself, drew my pictures that the adults did not understand and I watched over my baby brother.

The desire to create artistic things made me consider how to accomplish it around age three or four. I have no recollection of figuring out how to do it, but one day, I picked up a marker between my teeth and set about on the course of teaching myself to draw pictures like the other children were doing. I had no use of my hands, so I don't think anybody ever expected me to be able to write or draw. That prospect was never appealing to me. There were images in my mind that I needed to get out somehow and my instinct told me that artistic expression was something I knew very well. My mother followed the pediatrician's advice when he told her that I would have to find my own way in life. Accordingly, she let me make mistakes and get frustrated because it meant that I was learning my own limits. I could not accept that artistic pursuits were supposed to be listed among my limitations.

Drawing people quickly became my favorite thing to do but I never drew people from life. My family encouraged me to draw them from a very young age just to keep me practicing using writing utensils for when I started school. My grandmother in particular complained that I drew everybody "like those old black and white pictures that make everybody look stiff and dead." I had no idea what she meant because I had never been exposed to photographs of people outside of my immediate family. I thought I did something wrong, so I stopped drawing people from life altogether to keep myself from getting in trouble again, or so I thought was trouble.

Despite the complaint that I drew people like stiff old portraits, it became clear to my relatives that I had a gift for drawing people in a realistic way with soul that far exceeded my tender age. As time passed, the subjects of my crayon and marker drawings became repetitive to the point that my mother and grandmother thought they were people I knew. I said I did not know but I kept drawing the same types of images. One was a man with a dark blue suit and big black boots. The second was a woman with a sad, serious expression, dark hair and a big billowing skirt. The third person I drew was a younger woman with lighter hair, blue eyes and a sweet, mischievous smile.

I drew those people for years; the same pictures every time I sat down to doodle. It lasted well into my early teens, and by that time, I had taken to drawing the same profile of a woman with a dark bun at the nape of her neck. My teachers begged me to stop drawing in the margins of my notes and homework, but my mind wandered during class lectures and I compulsively wanted to draw the profile. A soothing feeling came over me when I got the features right; the line of her nose, the shape of his eyes, the color of their clothes. I felt compelled to draw them a certain way each time, as if looking at a portrait. My artistic subjects never smiled and the only one that ever looked away from the viewer was the dark-haired woman who turned her face downward, sadly.

I also had an obsessive desire to learn to read and write before I entered kindergarten. Literacy seemed like something necessary that I should have known since I was born, not that it was possible, but that was how my mind worked. Taking the time to learn things that everybody else seemed to know how to do frustrated me. Without understanding why, I thought things children did were a waste of time and I always wanted to be around adults and do adult things like writing letters, reading books and painting every piece of canvas I could find.

My desire to be so much like a grown woman before I even entered kindergarten gave my grandmother the impression that I was a stubborn and obstinate child. I had no point of reference for explaining what I went through because some knowledge is based on instinct rather than coherent thought. I was indeed a stubborn child who always managed to talk my way out of any sort of trouble whether I actually caused the trouble or not.

Perhaps one of the reasons I was so aware of everything around me was because my mother and father's marriage unraveled by the time my baby brother was nine-months-old. My father was a "functioning alcoholic," meaning he could be dangerously drunk at any given time but a person would never know it by looking at him. Soon after my parents separated, things were not going well financially for my mother. She tried to raise my brother and me with nothing but food stamps and a minimum wage job, and soon she feared the state removing us from her custody. Rather than see her children lost to foster homes, my mother made the painful decision to allow my aunt and uncle, who were childless, to adopt my two-year-old brother. I didn't see him again for eight years.

It could be suggested that my father's alcoholism, poverty and my brother's adoption caused some sort of psychological break from reality in me, which would be a satisfactory reason for some to refute my belief in reincarnation, but that is far from the truth. I have very little recollection of my father at all and what I do remember was not of a horrible drunk abusing his family. He simply was not around at all most of the time.

When my mother told me that my father was not living with us anymore, I remember thinking it was all right because I had already lost another daddy "before" and I survived it then too. I didn't cry. I didn't act out like many children do. I simply carried on with life. By the time I was four-years-old, my father was no longer a part of my life and I would not see him again until the divorce was finalized in about 1990. I never really missed my father because I was so young when he left and my mother's family became every type of parent that I needed over the years.

The phenomenon of toddler-aged children having spontaneous past life memories has no real bearing on what might be happening in their present lives. Children speaking openly about their past lives, albeit not consciously being aware of terms like "reincarnation" or "past lives," is only beginning to be studied and recorded in Western culture but has been commonly accepted for centuries in Eastern cultures.[2] While the concept of reincarnation is common and accepted in the East, only 25% of Americans over age eighteen polled in 2001 believe in reincarnation.[3] With such low statistics in the West, it is easy to see how small children in my position with spontaneous past life memories or strange unexplainable psychic abilities are encouraged very early on in their lives to fear and suppress their experiences.

I lived in Texas for a time, but at the age of six, I was sent away to live with my grandmother in St. Louis, Missouri, for a variety of reasons. My mother felt the education system in Texas was, at best, lacking proper motivation for teaching disabled students. She felt that St. Louis had a much better school system and she wanted to see me start off on the right foot with my education. My grandmother enrolled me into the Litzsinger School where many disabled children attended in that city.

Living with my grandmother quickly schooled me in an old-fashioned upbringing unlike the upbringing with which my mother raised me. My grandmother was of the generation that wrote letters, sent thank you cards, socialized in church, and children were to eat everything on their plates. "Waste not, want not" became

---

[2] Bowman, Carol, *Children's Past Lives: How Past Life Memories Affect Your Child*, Bantam Publishing (1998).

[3] 2001 US Gallup Organization.

the motto in our household. Since I was something of a stubborn child, I tested my limits with my grandmother at times.

I remember one night in particular, which has become something of family lore. That afternoon I spent on the living room floor practicing my letters because the teacher at school was unhappy with the old fashioned forms my letters took. My grandmother said supper was ready, so I stacked up my books and papers, and put all of the markers, pencils and crayons back in a Folgers coffee can. I was not hungry because I wanted to finish one of my watercolor paintings and I told her so. After a few bites of chicken and green beans, I backed away from the plate and declared that I was finished. Unflinching, my grandmother looked at me like I had sprouted another head and we stared each other down.

"Eat your supper," she said nonchalantly.

I reiterated that I was not hungry and I had better things to do. She finished her plate and left me with mine, saying that I was not allowed to do anything until I finished my food.

Ten minutes passed.

Then twenty.

Then an hour.

The food stared up at me from the plate in a cold pile of mush but neither my grandmother nor I were willing to back down. She was just as determined to see me finish the plate of food as I was determined not to finish it. As she lectured me about the starving children in Africa, a distinctly clear male voice overrode her lecture.

"Oh, you are a willful child! Now do as I ask or you will be confined to the house for the remainder of the day!"

The man's voice broke through my thoughts in such an invasive way that I thought it was a man on television. I looked over my shoulder expecting to see a man on the screen but the television was not even turned on. Silent, I considered what I heard and wondered if one of those see-through people was around in the house but I did not feel anything of that nature. It felt like a memory that I had not deliberately recalled. It felt forced on me.

The voice invading my thoughts startled me, not only in its severity but its familiarity. He sounded nothing like the men in my family and it unnerved me that I heard a threat of fatherly discipline in my mind when my father was a thousand miles away. His name seemed on the tip of my tongue but I couldn't quite grasp it and my frustration peaked for a split-second in a heavy sigh of defeat. I ate the chicken because of that voice. I knew he was a man that demanded obedience but how I knew that was a bigger mystery to me than who he was.

Being triggered by people or events that parallel the past is the most common way that spontaneous past life memories surface. Being reminded of the past event allows the deeply buried memories to be exposed and this cannot be controlled. Much of spontaneous past life memories come through the dream state but they can appear in the conscious state just as easily. The battle of wills between my grandmother and I most likely triggered the memory of a parental threat of discipline made by Fanny's adoptive father, Reverend Adams. He had a long history, I learned later, of being strict and critical of her even though they were as close as any father and daughter could be.

I spent a great deal of time in the St. Peter's Episcopal Church in St. Louis at my grandmother's side since my mother was not religious. My time in that church revolved around prayer, the hymnal, Heaven and Hell. My grandmother was my biggest religious influence as a child, although my mother encouraged me to question life, ideas and teachings on every subject. My mother encouraged me to choose religious principles that felt right to me and not just choose the Episcopal Church because it was the church of my childhood. Those lessons of self-exploration also motivated my mother to refrain from discussing her own beliefs, which were far different than those of the church of my childhood. She believed I should discover things for myself.

As I grew, I did question a lot of what I was taught, especially when the things I experienced were not real in the eyes of ministers and authority figures in my life. I found God in beauty and felt that my gifts of seeing people who have died or my gifts in art or literacy or anything else in my existence were blessed and inspired by God. I wondered why church had to be the designated place to speak to God when His hand created all of the beauty in nature and gave people the intelligence to improve upon it. Even from that young age, my feelings were naturally more liberal and nearly Transcendentalist without knowing what Transcendentalism was. Eventually, I shifted to the Catholic Church, although my beliefs evolved into a liberal potpourri of several different faiths, both Eastern and Western.

My rebelliousness against the expectations of others and my feelings of being "odd" were consistent with factors that shaped Fanny's belief system. Her family was deeply entrenched in the strict Congregationalist faith, but for reasons similar to my own, she could not reconcile herself to the strict conservatism and never officially joined the Congregational church. She was far more liberal and it caused friction between her and some members of her family. Like me, she found God in everything, questioned things she was taught, and believed so many gifts in art, life, and so on, were offered from God. She attended Unitarian churches occasionally in her travels, which, at that time, was considered one of the most liberal and scandalous church in the country.

Most Americans of the nineteenth century adhered to Calvinist leanings of Christianity that included the trinity of God, believing that Jesus Christ was His physical divine incarnation, as well as the Bible being the literal Word of God. In Calvinist belief, each person was born with Original Sin. What made the Unitarian church so threatening to people was the belief in the oneness of God and that Jesus Christ was not divine. He was an example of morality and possibly a prophet of God, but they firmly believed God was a singular holy being. They believed people were capable of both good and evil through the exercise of free will and were not born with the corruption of Original Sin. Unitarianism connected to Transcendentalism through notable figures like Ralph Waldo Emerson with the common belief that philosophy, science, rationality and self-insight were meant to coexist with faith in God.[4] Fanny embracing ideas so different from the strictness of her

---

[4] Henderson, A.C., *What Do Unitarians Believe?* (AUA, 1866).

father and husband's church caused friction within the family for most of her life, although her husband accepted her beliefs as well-considered.

The parallel of my basic beliefs with Fanny's, as I uncovered them later in life, comforted me because I understood that my oddities were not sudden. I was not born into this life with that sort of rebellion appearing from nowhere. It seems to be a natural progression of a soul that naturally questions things to reach deeper into the heart of life and find truth for myself.

By the time I entered the first grade at Ross Elementary School in St. Louis, I had a long list of inexplicable dreams about Fanny's life filed away, but my childlike mind had no point of reference to make sense of them. I had become fairly convinced that a handful of people were haunting me, having learned what ghosts were that Halloween, but I was too embarrassed to tell anyone about it. I kept the dreams tucked away inside myself as a place of comfort to visit that no one else could see. I knew the faces of those the mysterious woman loved just as I knew my own family. I knew their voices, their laughter and their tears. I just didn't know that one of them was me.

CHAPTER THREE

On my first day of the first grade, a teacher for disabled children broke my leg in a random accident. I had a lunchtime bathroom break and the teacher needed my wheelchair to be closer to the toilet so she pushed the headgear that operated the wheelchair. Abruptly, my wheelchair lurched headlong into a metal bathroom shelf directly in my path. Shooting agony immediately sucked all the breath from my lungs for a moment until I let out a blood-curdling scream. At the emergency room that evening, my mother and grandmother stood by my bedside as the doctor incorrectly declared there was no break in the bone and I simply needed a week's worth of rest.

That night with my swollen, bruised leg propped on a series of pillows, I experienced my first nightmare from Fanny's life – a nightmare with has haunted me periodically through my present life.

I stood in the woman's body, the woman I did not know, yet she distinctly felt like me. Night air curled around outside but I stood inside of a sparse, hot tent watching five men talk in agitated voices around another man who was lying down in the middle of them. Two of the men had foreign accents. I felt an antsy ball in the pit of my stomach and compulsively squeezed my hands together. As I looked closer at the man lying down, a feeling overwhelmed me that the limp body was my husband. He did not appear to be fully conscious but he was not unconscious either. Blood stained the blanket partially fallen on the ground from his body.

One of the foreigners looked at me and all five of them started poking and prodding at his body, torturing him. The way it seemed to my seven-year-old mind, this was torture, but they were, in actuality, trying to help him. As they worked on him, he made terrible sounds of agony and the helplessness I felt made tears spill from my eyes. In my extreme anxiety, I lunged forward to try and stop the men. Two more men grabbed me by the arms and pulled me back.

"Stop! You'll kill him!" I screamed.

My voice was not my own, though it had similar tone and felt quite natural at the time. She sounded more melodic and lyrical than I do now, even in her deep state of fright. Her anguish was so present in me that I thought I might die too, had I not woken as if being jerked from her body.

Awake suddenly, it took a moment to regain my senses and remember where I was. Tears and cold sweat dampened my pillow as I cried out for my mother, unable to shake the fright of a grown woman facing the prospect of watching her husband die. My mother rushed to my bedside thinking that I had injured my leg further but once she established that my leg was not the cause, she became more agitated because I refused to tell her what had me so upset. I was only in the first grade, after all, and I couldn't begin to explain my dreams if I didn't understand them.

That night's dream was certainly not the first dream I had been through about the other family who lived in old clothes, but it was by far the most intense. Before that, I had dreamed a few times about being a little girl saying goodbye to her father and wondering why I was not going home with him. Otherwise, only a few minor activities had triggered my mind, like the taste of certain foods or the aroma of certain flowers. It was nothing I couldn't handle or even paid much attention to, until I began dreaming about the husband who had been shot and could have died right in front of me. As the nightmare repeated itself, I began to fear the possibility that I really would have to watch him die, not knowing the facts behind the situation.

Many years later, I learned there was a lot of truth in that recurring nightmare. The man who might have died had, in fact, been my husband, who was shot through the pelvis and nearly killed in the early stages of the Siege of Petersburg, Virginia, at a place called Rives' Salient. Fanny had gone immediately to the naval hospital in Annapolis to nurse him through what everyone thought were his last days. The two foreign men remained a mystery for me for years until I found that the head of the hospital was an immigrant from Holland named Vanderkieft who learned English upon arriving in America just before the Civil War and most certainly had a heavy accent.[5] Much later in his life, Lawrence made a vague reference in an essay about the wounding about a Welshman. It is possible for that vague reference to indicate the second man with an accent, although it cannot completely be documented.[6] Lawrence had become something of a guinea pig for experimental procedures, including metal catheters that probably caused a painful fistula present for the remainder of his life.[7] One can only imagine the horrors Fanny witnessed done to him in the name of medical science. In that life, I had lived in an adjoining tent looking after him for part of the summer of 1864 and on top of everything, I was pregnant with our last child to be born the following January.

Petersburg has been a forbidden subject for me since I was four or five-years-old. My uncle was the first person I remember uttering the word and it clamped my stomach like a vice grip. I never wanted to feel that fear again. Even today, knowing the cause of my fears, I still cannot easily speak openly about the summer of 1864. Occasionally I experience shadowy images of that dreadful tent beyond the nightmare but they are so fleeting and gut-wrenching for me that I almost instantly bury them as soon as they bubble from my subconscious.

A great number of people with past life memories are introduced to those lives through the traumatic events they suffered at the time. Going through just one experience in my memory of the awful summer of 1864 jolted me and forced me to sit up and take notice. The previous glimpses of that life were so minor and

---

[5] Vanderkieft obituary published in the *NY Times* on September 16, 1866.

[6] Smith, Diane Monroe, *Chamberlain at Petersburg: The Charge at Fort Hell, June 18, 1864*, (Thomas Publications, 2004).

[7] Smith, Diane Monroe, *Fanny and Joshua: The Enigmatic Lives of Frances Caroline Adams and Joshua Lawrence Chamberlain*, (Thomas Publications, 1999).

fleeting that I barely acknowledged them at all, but after that nightmare, the initial question of why this was happening started to form. My natural heightened awareness of things both spiritual and physical made me wonder if the see-through people were telling me things about themselves. However, after I started school, I began ignoring those people. Even after I suppressed my child mediumship, the dreams persisted in such a personal way that it felt like cutting open very old and painful scars inside of me. I felt like it was me going through those things, but without someone to teach me about reincarnation, it would be years before I understood.

The small questions forming in my mind about why I had such bizarre dreams might have knocked loose more pieces of the wall blocking my past from my present. At times, the most minuscule activities made me have flashes of things in the past as if recalling something from just a week ago. It wasn't just happening in the dream state anymore by the end of the first grade. I baked a lot with my grandmother, as most grandchildren do, but there were times sitting by the counter in my wheelchair that I would have flashes of standing in a long heavy dress doing things at a wooden kitchen table in an entirely different kitchen.

The sensation of standing and using my hands like anyone else was probably the most unnerving aspect about those occasional dreams or waking flashbacks. I had never been able to walk in my life and doctors said that I never would walk, yet I knew the specific details of how to stand and the sensation of walking across a room. If I had never walked on my own, then how was it that I could dream so realistically about the act? It frightened me at times – knowing how to write with my hand, or how to wash dishes, or how to change cloth diapers, but the inexplicable knowledge of walking, running or simply standing got to me the most.

As far as I knew, nobody in my family suspected the complex things going on in my mind. I went to great lengths to hide it because if nobody else contemplated their dreams or things they couldn't control in their thoughts, then it must not be normal. I only drew the people in those memories when my family wasn't watching and I avoided it altogether at school because I noticed right away that the other children didn't even know how to draw things like that, let alone what they were. The profile of the woman with the dark bun at the nape of her neck was the only sketch I allowed myself in the margins of my homework papers. I copied the rainbows, animals and things that my classmates were drawing in an effort to fit in with the crowd. Being stared at because of my disability and then later because of my artistic skill made me extremely uncomfortable with any extra attention.

First grade ended with my mother finding a new husband and reclaiming custody of me from my grandmother. As we prepared for her to come to St. Louis, she sent me a box of toys so I would know that I was not forgotten. One of the toys was a doll that looked like a newborn baby and I got extremely attached to it immediately. I treated that doll as if it was a real baby, which was not at all unlike other children of that age, but the doll looked, to me, like a real baby in my dreams before it was ever given to me.

In the middle of the night, I woke up several times thinking there was a baby in a cradle in the room with me that needed attention but clearly there was not. There was an incident in which I'd had a dream that I was holding a tiny dark-haired baby who was fussing and crying, and being worried about the baby's fever. There were male voices talking in another part of the house and I felt guilt for not being out there with them but the baby needed me more. As soon as I woke up, I woke my grandmother too and demanded to know why the baby hadn't been seen by a doctor yet. She didn't have a clue of what I was talking about and did her best to soothe me by telling me it was just a bad dream. The lingering worry I felt for the baby in my arms lasted for days.

My grandmother interpreted my quiet mood as being afraid of the changes with my mother remarrying, so she planned a few special things for me to take my mind off of it. One of those afternoon excursions was a trip to an arts and crafts festival in the park by the Gateway Arch and the Mississippi River. Since we had moved to St. Louis, I had adored going to the river and sitting in the grass watching the boats go by. As we walked by the water, I felt happy, relaxed and I thought nothing about school, my family or my dreams.

Happily, I closed my eyes and breathed in the warm, humid Mississippi River air. In that darkness, shapes and colors unfolded until I saw another river, narrower, in the place of the Mississippi. I heard all the tourists, cars and street noise around me perfectly well, but the quieter vision of an undeveloped riverbank spread out before me with tall grass and a scattering of wildflowers. I looked down at myself and saw not a wheelchair but a long brown skirt with paisley strips and I felt my legs treading along underneath it. I knew what it was then, having long since grown accustomed to this woman invading my life at the most inopportune moments.

I looked back over my shoulder and there was the wounded man from the old nightmare, much younger and strong. I almost didn't recognize him because he had a beard instead of a mustache but the twinkling blue eyes looking right through me spoke clearly of who it was. He faithfully walked behind me with a small wooden chest under one arm and a folded artist's easel under the other arm. A smile parted his lips and a thought in her voice came through clear as daylight with a peaceful, happy sensation radiating, it seemed, straight from my chest.

"He loves me."

Of course, I could not understand the depth of her feeling since I was such a young child. The one thing I could interpret from it was that she had realized that he loved her for the first time at that moment and it made her happy but she was not ready to voice it yet. Why on earth anyone would fear being truly happy, I could not understand though. I felt extremely adult love wrapped up in many other inexplicable emotions for my age even though boys at school hadn't begun to interest me yet. So I began to take more curiosity in solving the mystery than passively waiting for more visions. If I was meant to feel what she felt, I wanted to know exactly who she was. It was only fair.

The school had gotten together with my mother and decided that I was not with the right age group because my intelligence was ahead of the children in my class. I skipped the second grade and went directly from the first grade to the third grade. I saw it as an opportunity to start over again and to be perfectly normal in the eyes of my peers. Moving back home with my mother and starting over with new classmates excited me.

I became so adept at acting like everybody else that I started to believe it too. I had sleepovers with girls from school; we read magazines, dressed like Debbie Gibson and Tiffany, traded posters of New Kids on the Block, Joey Lawrence, Jonathan Brandis and so many other popular teen idols at that time. My favorite place to be was Chesterfield Mall, mainly because I could watch other kids there and figure out how to be more like everybody else. Despite my best efforts to run with the crowd, my friends still poked fun at me sometimes because I read voraciously, wrote poetry, short stories and painted whenever I could. Third graders didn't do those things very much but I wouldn't give up on them.

Despite my best efforts to simply be a child, I could not suppress every dream. The frequency had stalled by the time I was halfway through that school year but one dream stuck with me in nearly the same way the dream about the sick baby had. In all of the experiences with Fanny that I went through, I had never seen what she looked like physically because I went through everything within that body. It was my own body, after all. I walked through a narrow hallway in the dream, toward a door leading to the front yard, and toward the end of the hall, there was a mirror hanging on the wall with hooks for hats and coats. I stopped there to put on a pair of dark-colored gloves and then I looked up to my reflection in the mirror as I tied a dark blue bonnet under my chin. I looked tired, haggard and there was a sense of deep sadness about me.

There was terrible sadness hidden in my eyes as Fanny but I stood at that mirror with my shoulders back and a cool, fearless mask over my face. Just as I was in the present as a little girl, I guarded myself carefully as Fanny, it seemed. I smoothed the dark hair over my temple and a strong sense of déjà vu fell over me. The way I wrinkled my forehead mimicked the way I do it now. The way my mouth thinned in concentration mimicked the way it does now. Even the colors I wore as Fanny were colors I choose for myself now.

The shock of looking at myself in a different body, yet still feeling distinctly like me, was more than I could bear and I woke up suddenly, heart pounding and mind swimming. As Fanny, I was taller than I am now but not by much (I'm five feet tall) and my figure was much more like an hourglass carefully shaped by a corset. The eyes I had in the dream were the most shocking aspect because they were brown when I have dull blue-gray eyes now. Colors may change from life to life, I have noticed, but looking into my formerly brown eyes or looking into my blue eyes in the mirror has the same familiarity. A person always recognizes themselves in images and I recognized myself in that different, perfectly able body while I slept in the confines of a quadriplegic body.

Still, I did my best to ignore it when things like that happened. My childhood came to a slow ending as the years of school advanced into junior high and much to my relief, the dreams and waking flashbacks slowed to a trickle. If it took me pretending to be like everyone else in order to make it stop, then I intended to pretend until I conditioned myself enough that the new me was the authentic me. Sometimes the old me reemerged unintentionally, such as when I was integrated into an advanced reading and writing program, or I revealed a natural aptitude for history. My first exposure in school to the Civil War came as a rather brief lesson in the sixth grade. I never studied. I simply knew what happened. I had looked at my uncle's Civil War books as a young child before I could read and I felt the strangest déjà vu about the period but I was not educated in it.

As much as I tried to fit in, I could not deny my voracious appetite for art and books. Instead of playing on the playground equipment, I hid in quiet corners reading every book I could obtain from the library. First I drifted to the classics by authors Nathaniel Hawthorne and Louisa May Alcott and the librarian suggested that I look at the history books in the nonfiction part of the library. I started with picture books about the Civil War but the thought of reading about troop numbers, movements and old men in uniforms bored me into unconsciousness so I avoided it. The pictures drew me in, however. Some of the faces and names looked so familiar but I could never place them. My choice for books perplexed my classmates and the more they saw me with them, the more alienated

I became, except for a few close friends. When I read Civil War books, the children giggled and called me an old lady. When I read Gothic books like Bram Stoker's or Edgar Allen Poe's work, the children giggled and called me Stephen King's ghostly secret daughter.

I could not seem to win no matter what I did. If I pretended to be like everybody else and ignore the fact that I felt and saw spirit apparitions since I was a baby or ignore the fact that I had dreams and flashes of being in someone else's body, I couldn't pretend to be non-artistic or uninterested in books. Soon I began to realize that I was never going to be "like everybody else" and I was not going to have an easy time of making friends. People appeared to be amazed by my artistic abilities and any kind of adulation made me uncomfortable. If there was too much attention on me, I just knew people were going to figure out the secrets I carried my entire life. The thought of being exposed periodically became so intense that I quit painting or drawing for months and sometimes years at a time. Being uncomfortable in my own skin was my version of real normalcy.

In the summer of 1995, my family and I made the journey from St. Louis to Atlanta to visit family. As a thirteen-year-old girl, the furthest thing from my mind was contemplating the great mysteries of life and death, but my first exposure to the Chamberlain myth happened during that trip, leaving a mark on me for the rest of my life. My uncle had plans to take my mother and her husband out for the night and since I was not old enough to go to bars, I stayed with the neighbor.

My uncle offered to rent a movie, to which I offhandedly remarked, "Anything about the Civil War is fine." He rented *Gettysburg,* based on the novel *The Killer Angels* by Michael Shaara, which was based on the three days of bloody fighting between the Union and Confederate armies in July of 1863. One of the main characters profiled in the film was Joshua Lawrence Chamberlain, Colonel of the 20th Maine Volunteer Infantry Regiment. I found the film difficult to follow because most of my self-education about the Civil War had focused on simplistic picture books, domestic and family topics, completely avoiding combat or military aspects.

The only parts of the film that occupied my interest were the scenes in which Jeff Daniels and C. Thomas Howell portrayed Colonel Chamberlain and his younger brother, Tom, respectively. A sense of distant familiarity churned in the pit of my stomach, although I could not understand why. Some things about the actors felt wrong, despite the foggy sensation of having heard the story of Gettysburg many, many times in the past.

Distant familiarity reached its crescendo in the climactic scene for the Chamberlain brothers as they fought the 15th Alabama on the peak known as Little Round Top. The 20th Maine found itself running out of ammunition to fight off the Confederate regiments, and in a moment of desperation and bravery, Jeff Daniels as Colonel Chamberlain drew in a sharp breath and bellowed, "Bayonet!"

Immediately, the words fell out of my mouth, "It didn't happen that way!"

I had no idea why that phrase sprang from my lips, considering I knew almost nothing about the tactical elements of the Battle of Gettysburg. My uncle's neighbor asked what I meant and I could not find an answer to explain my reaction. I looked at the television screen again and felt my stomach knot up in fear. What was I afraid of in a simple movie?

For a time, I forced myself to fit in with normal society as my adolescence developed but it was to be short-lived. The pieces of me inside that once were Fanny Chamberlain, wife of that colonel on Little Round Top, began to kick and claw their way to the surface. It became a battle – the more I denied her, the bigger the fight she put up to be discovered and acknowledged.

CHAPTER FOUR

Blessedly, as a teenager, it was finally cool and acceptable to read and write poetry, short stories and novels, as long as a person went with that crowd. The people I grew up with appeared to have a grasp on the fact that I wasn't going to change and that I could be an artist, a writer and a fun friend to keep around. Boys eluded me, although I moved from one flirtation to another. In general, I felt boys were childish with no real depth and I preferred older age groups, much to my mother's anxiety.

My mother was passed over for a promotion that she deserved at her job and she quit that job with lofty dreams of starting our life over again in a small town. So, after I finished my sophomore year of high school, she uprooted me from everything I knew and moved me southward to a small town in northwest Georgia. Being in completely unfamiliar surroundings elevated my anxiety so much that I no longer had control over my dreams and the spiritual sensitivity I exhibited as a small child came rushing back with a vengeance. Still, we had family in Calhoun and my mother wanted me to have the small town upbringing that she had while I was still young enough to be impacted by it. The one bright spot in the move was that I would finally have a relationship with my brother beyond letters.

Almost immediately after moving to Calhoun, I began having dreams about being in and around a smaller version of a stereotypical plantation house with white columns. I hadn't seen that house in any other dreams of my brown-eyed alter-ego but I was too upset about the move away from St. Louis to really care. To me, everything about Georgia represented separation and depression borne of being almost a complete foreigner to the people there.   Several years later, I discovered that the stereotypical plantation house had been one where Fanny lived when she lived in Georgia.   She had taken a job as a music teacher in Milledgeville in an independent showing that she could pay off her music school and family debts before she married Lawrence.   My move to Georgia was not only a parallel to Fanny's life but it triggered brief flashes of her time there.

I found it difficult to make friends in Georgia, not only as a transplanted Yankee, but as someone who found Southern religious values baffling and foreign.   Questions like, "When were you saved?" and, "Which church do you belong to?" were never questions I encountered in St. Louis.   The subject of religion had always been a private one for me and I found it difficult to comprehend how religion was such an open topic as if it was the center of the Southern universe.   To me, discussing my religion with perfect strangers felt like exposing a part of myself that would leave me open to attacks, strange looks and unfair judgment.   I was fanatical about protecting the knowledge of the nineteenth century family buried in my subconscious to the point of hiding it from my family and friends.

I completely alienated myself in the eyes of my peers by accident in the first few months at my new high school.   The history teacher assigned a project of making family trees, which I thought was going to be fun.   I came from a mixed family of German, French Huguenot, English and more than one tribe of Native American heritage.   I'm also related to General William Tecumseh Sherman and Maine author Sarah Orne Jewett, both of which I found through doing the school project.   Being related to General Sherman, who was blamed in the South for burning his way through Georgia during the Civil War, was the kiss of death for me. The teacher posted our family trees in the hallway outside of the classroom and I was never able to make real, lasting friendships after that.   I had no idea that the war was not over for those people, especially when some told me things like, "Your family burned my family's farm."   So in Calhoun, I was my own friend for the most part, although I had one friend who overlooked my differences with Southern society and became like a sister to me.

During my first year in Calhoun, I still had no concept of reincarnation, although I was fully aware of what it meant to be a ghost. That was my own diagnosis for the problem of "knowing" my nineteenth century family. I had seen a television show a few years before in which a child who saw ghosts was profiled. The mother explained that the child had been blocking what he saw and that appeared to make the problem go away. A light bulb lit up for me then because I had been blocking on instinct. I did not know that blocking was a known method for dealing with those things. I made an art form out of suppression again, and by the time I began my second year in Georgia, suppressing my dreams and visions had become a habit.

Nobody told me that suppressing natural intuitive or medium abilities could cause great harm to a person's mental condition. Nobody told me that in order to let go of past life memories, had I even known what they were, they had to be acknowledged and dealt with directly, in most cases. I never made the connection that trying to pretend that part of me did not exist marked the beginning of the most severe period of depression and anxiety in my life. At any given moment after having a dream or having a thought connected to those people, if I had acknowledged it and found a cause for it, I could have avoided years of self-loathing and fear. Instead, I continued to ignore it and behave like a normal teenager.

Georgia, I learned quickly, was a place deeply invested in and in love with its history. It seemed to have been a running joke that the Civil War never ended and the reenacting culture was far more prevalent there than in St. Louis. I felt compelled almost immediately to become part of it, despite an intense phobia of guns and cannons. My phobia has been a debilitating presence in my life since I was a baby and it affects me so deeply that I find even fireworks on the Fourth of July or the sound of a balloon popping absolutely terrifying. I equate the sounds of explosions with imminent death of those I love. The intense desire to reenact the Civil War period has always been at poignant odds with my phobia. The two fixed points of who I am fight each other until I cannot contain it anymore and the battle manifests as panic attacks.

Still, I participated in and was a spectator at Civil War reenactments all over northwest Georgia. When people ask why I put myself through the torture of guns and cannons, I never know how to respond other than, "I have to do it."

Civil War reenacting from the lady's perspective was like a healing awareness for me. Some things I knew by instinct, such as how to breathe in a corset without getting lightheaded or the way I seemed to have a knack for seeing what was inaccurate about someone's attire or portrayal. I realized quickly that wearing the proper clothing and being immersed in the reenactments, which were like massive outdoor theatrical experiences, boosted my confidence and offered me a feeling of being "home" again. I was the only female that I knew who was eager to spend weekends wearing layers of clothing in the blazing Georgia sun with people two or three times my age. There was no way for me to comprehend why I felt so at home in restrictive corsets and billowing skirts.

At the end of my junior year of high school, the self-imposed block I had on my nineteenth century family dislodged itself in a traumatic series of dreams. Again I found myself, as I termed it, sucked into the body of the woman with heavy dark hair and a heavy black dress, seated beside a coffin. An infant lay in that coffin and as I became more immersed in the surroundings, the pain of knowing that baby was mine struck like slamming headlong into a brick wall. My chest constricted, my stomach rolled with violent nausea and my hands ached from squeezing a handkerchief so tight.

Thrust into extremely painful feelings of motherly grief, I knew consciously that it was a dream but I couldn't pull myself out of it. It felt like I had gone from zero to sixty in seconds of paralyzing sorrow and it was nothing short of having one foot in the past and one foot in the present. I sat as still as stone in that old chair because if I moved at all, the grip on my composure would break. I watched people talking in hushed voices and wanted them out of my house. In the background, the man who had long since felt like my husband stood by a window, one hand on the wall, the other in his pocket, and a vacant expression as if he had no awareness of people around him. Every cell in my body fought the urge to fall on the floor weeping and pounding my fists on the floorboards until the anger dissipated.

"Lord, sustain me. I cannot endure this again," I thought with my other voice before I finally pulled myself out of it.

The dream repeated itself periodically for years and I found it frightening, not because there was a monster chasing me in the dark, but because I could not get a handle on grief that deep at my young age. I was old enough to understand motherhood but nobody could understand the agony of losing a child unless they went through it firsthand. I felt guilty for assuming I understood the grief of a mother through that dream even though I had no children of my own. On top of that, I still occasionally had dreams of being in army hospitals and seeing blood and the man I later knew as Joshua Lawrence Chamberlain put through the most painful things, which were intensely frightening because I did not understand them. Those dreams stuck with me for days afterward and affected my day-to-day moods and mental condition. Sometimes I wouldn't go back to sleep afterward or I avoided going to sleep in the first place, which left me exhausted at school during the day.

I wanted the double life in my conscious and subconscious to stop. I went as far as pleading with what I assumed to be the ghost of this woman to go on to Heaven and leave me alone. Nothing seemed to relieve the pressure. I became more and more withdrawn from my family and friends; often spending hours secluded in my bedroom because I did not understand why I appeared to be the only one enduring such spontaneous and unwelcome visions.

I took an interest in the paranormal in rather broad terms, in my quest to stop what was happening to me. I was rather clueless about the inner workings of spirituality, ghosts, the afterlife and the like, beyond what I had learned in the church of my childhood. Lack of guidance opened the door for me to dabble in potentially dangerous activities such as consulting an Ouija board on occasion and I also began teaching myself to use Tarot cards. I researched different religions such as Wicca and Ancient Egyptian mysticism. For a brief period, I rejected my Episcopal upbringing in favor of adopting the Egyptian goddess Isis as my own patron saint of protection. I chose her after I read that her husband, Osiris, was the god of the underworld. My goal in all of this was to banish or even exorcise the nineteenth century family from my subconscious mind.

Conversely, within a year I thoroughly rejected polytheism, most likely due to the nearly oppressive Christian air hanging over my Southern home. Nobody I knew researched other religious beliefs and my quest for answers gave way to the desire to be like everyone else – to simply be another sheep in the herd. I became outwardly ultraconservative, vowing such things as virginity until marriage, absolute faith in God, belief in angels and demons, etc. Despite my outward change of attitude, I continued my introverted struggle. Not even blind faith in God could help me understand why I had to be the one experiencing vignettes and images of the family who lived in an entirely different century.

Disbelief gave way to depression. Depression gave way to anxiety and fear. Anxiety and fear gave way to anger. I slowly began to realize that I was the only one who could make the dreams and visions stop. I could not depend on anyone but myself. Instead of banishing the family from my thoughts, I slowly began analyzing the things I saw and I decided that step one of my uncharted plan would be to discover the woman's identity.

CHAPTER FIVE

As I prepared to enter my senior year of high school in 1999, I allowed myself to feel a false sense of peace. A plan was comforting in a small way but I knew I would not reap the fruits of that plan until I figured out how to go about identifying the people in my subconscious. Rarely did they speak to each other and I had not heard any names. Most of my dreams and visions were short snippets based almost exclusively on residual thought, emotion and visual cues. All I had to go on were glimpses of buildings unfamiliar to me in the present and the sound of a bizarre accent peppered with soft R's and odd phraseology that I had not heard before, yet I always understood in the moment.

Spontaneous past life memories do not come with a timestamp or a tour guide to explain what one might be feeling, seeing or experiencing. Time is not a linear concept to the soul and therefore, the memories will manifest out of chronological order on what appears to be a need-to-know basis. I had originally thought that the man I later identified as Joshua Lawrence Chamberlain was more than one man because his appearance changed frequently, and for quite a few years, I only had brief but meaningful glimpses of him. At times, his facial hair was arranged as long sideburns, or a full beard, or what I call an Amish beard, or the great drooping mustache most familiar to history. In addition, he had three brothers, so I could have easily seen them as well. It is incredibly difficult and time-consuming to try to break down spontaneous past life memories and make sense out of the events being shown.

Although I still approached the "old family" as a ghostly problem and not a reincarnation one, I began noticing certain events in my life corresponded with certain visions of the woman's life. For example, when my father disappeared from my life at the age of four, I experienced one of my first spontaneous memories. From within Fanny's own four-year-old body, I went through the moment when it began to dawn on her that her birth father, Ashur Adams, was not going to allow her to come home. She had been given to Ashur's nephew, Reverend George Adams, for adoption because her own family was too impoverished to feed another child. I, as a present four-year-old, felt paralleling sorrow and rejection with the four-year-old in 1829.

Such moments I now term as "memory triggers," when an event or profound emotion parallels with an event or profound emotion one experienced in a past life. Most people experience a sense of déjà vu, while others, like me, literally see the past events as tools in order to learn a lesson that had not been learned in the past.

My belief that the "old family" was somehow haunting me could not explain certain intense feelings I experienced within the woman's body. They felt as familiar to me as my own emotions, yet she went through things that I never could have understood in my seventeen years. Love for her children was eternal and the silent endurance when three of them were buried before their first birthdays left wounds in her that would never heal.

Aside from the powerful love and devotion to her children, one thing I knew for certain was the ardent love she felt for her husband. It was so present in her mind, body and soul that she found it overpowering at times, which made her shrink away and become guarded and introverted about it. Too much of any emotion made her nervous, which is a trait that carried over into who I am today. Since I could not explain why her emotions felt distinctly like my own, I found myself shrinking away from those thoughts and pretending as if they were not happening. Feeling so emotionally invested in her life as if it were my own did not fit with my conclusion that she was a ghostly entity haunting me, so I ignored anything that did not fit with my theories.

Everything was turned upside down just before I began my senior year of high school. My mother took me to a local chain bookstore for a little shopping, as I was an avid reader. The shopping expedition began rather uneventfully but as I browsed the history section, one book in particular caught my eye. It sat wedged between two books as heavy as encyclopedias but it caught my eye because the words "Fanny & Joshua" were scrawled on the spine, giving it the look of a romance novel. Intrigued, I asked for the book to be brought down for a closer look. The clerk casually mentioned that someone had ordered the book a few weeks prior but never appeared to collect it.

My eyes fell on the dark red cover with two oval-shaped images of a man and a woman. The words on the cover blurred and my forehead suddenly felt damp with anxiousness. I knew the mustache on the man's face. I knew the shape of his nose, his jaw and the way his hair swooped across his head. My eyes shifted up to the profile photograph of the woman and I felt myself try to swallow but the muscles of my throat were paralyzed. I knew her. She was the same woman I had seen in the mirror in my dream when I was in the third grade. I knew her thoughts, her emotions, her love for the man in the oval next to her, her insecurities, her sense of being misunderstood.

"Do you want this one?" my mother asked.

"No," I blurted, surprising myself.

I wanted to get as far away from that book as I could. My mind and body reeled with a similar feeling a person experienced just stepping off of a roller coaster. The book was called *Fanny and Joshua: The Enigmatic Lives of Frances Caroline Adams and Joshua Lawrence Chamberlain*, written by Diane Monroe Smith.

The ghost had a name. Fanny. She was real. Not only was she real but deep down I knew she was not a ghost at all. She was me and I was her and those people I had been seeing since I was a toddler were once my family. Something inside of me cracked and I found myself unable to catch my breath, although I pulled every ounce of strength to appear calm and collected. I passed off my reaction as being overheated and I asked to be taken outside for some fresh air.

The clerk put the book back on the shelf as I was taken outside, numb and dumbfounded, and I refused to look at it again for almost four years.

CHAPTER SIX

How does one cope with reincarnation when they have just realized it exists and it isn't a fabrication of Hollywood or novelists? Some people want the mystery. Some people want the oddity and the notoriety that comes with documentable or non-documentable cases. Just as with any other type of fame, some people crave the attention whether it's positive or negative.

I was not one of those people. I wanted nothing to do with it, especially after my traumatizing trip to the bookstore. The faces on that book cover haunted me for weeks afterward and I withdrew back into myself once more. My personal frustration could not be articulated to those who wondered what was wrong with me but even I became annoyed with my silence and my sour moods. A distinctly real fear trickled into me that somebody might stumble onto the truth that I could not even admit to myself. I did not touch a Civil War book at all for months because I did not want to risk seeing his face or reading some string of words that might trigger more unwelcome visions.

Natural questions surfaced in my mind but there was nobody who could answer them. Was I crazy? Why me? Did everybody else have similar experiences? Why was I supposed to remember a past life? What was I supposed to do with it?

I could not accept that something so profound could happen to me by a random twist of fate, yet I had no example to follow about how I was supposed to wade through such a murky and hidden subject. I knew I could not talk to a psychiatrist about it. A psychiatrist would simply put me on anti-anxiety medication at the minimum or go as far as to diagnose me with a serious mental illness like schizophrenia or multiple personality disorder. In either event, a stigma would be attached to me that I could never handle in front of other people. How was I supposed to believe in something that the whole of Western society thought was nothing but make believe?

Yet there were instances over the following months when I would see a man on the street with piercing blue eyes like the eyes I knew "before," or I would hear a piece of old piano music, or hear a baby's cry, and a deeply buried part of me began to ache. The fear I felt over being "found out" never truly faded but a hollow sensation in the pit of my soul took over in time. Denying Fanny's life felt as painful as denying my present life including all of the people in it. I gradually began to wonder if my soul had left her body to occupy this present body, then who else from her life occupied new bodies? What was the larger purpose?

I found it difficult, after graduating high school, to ignore my growing interest in Joshua Lawrence Chamberlain. When I was certain nobody would see me, I began reading about him on the Internet. Bit by bit, piece by piece, little things I read about him clicked with things I had known about the man in my dreams. At times, I felt like I was sneaking behind my parents' backs to get to know that man and the remnants of Fanny within wanted to look at his photographs and learn more.

I found it difficult to explain the feeling of residual love for a man who had been dead and buried since 1914. The eighteen-year-old girl inside of me found it completely repugnant that I could find a man from an entirely different century attractive but I reluctantly admitted to myself that I did. He had been flesh and blood once. Grainy sepia images simply did not do him justice but never would I admit such a thing beyond my own private thoughts.

While I struggled to explain residual feelings of love for a man long gone, I also could not bring myself to read about Fanny or even look at her photographs. If I saw her name in text, I skipped over it and even felt hatred for her. Two years of hatred toward Fanny filled the empty spaces between missing who Lawrence was (I had begun thinking of him as Lawrence), the sound of his voice and the million other little things often described by widows. I felt like a widow at times, even though I grew to hate the woman who was his wife. I became vocal about hating Fanny to a few trusted friends and I went as far as suggesting the possibility that Lawrence was unfaithful to her because she was described by historians as cold and unfeeling.

Hating Fanny was easier than becoming the target of historians who felt she was unworthy of a man of Lawrence's stature and character.

Hating Fanny allowed me the outlet to express my anger over the entire situation without drawing attention to myself.

Although I struggled in silence with coming to terms with my previous life, my present life was never neglected. I graduated high school with a near-perfect grade point average and I decided on teaching as a career path, though I was undecided about whether I would teach art or history. My artistic skills developed and my pieces were displayed in various art shows throughout the Southeast.

I kept up relationships with a few close friends but I never shared my struggle with them. Even within my long-term relationship with a man, I kept it a secret, and it weighed heavily on my shoulders because we had a very open and honest relationship. He was something of an atheist and it was an area of our relationship where we met with mutual respect and agreed to disagree. I could never have realistically expected him to understand what I was going through if he did not even believe in God.

In a way, I escaped into my present life if only to avoid having to deal with my past life, which is quite the opposite of what happens to a lot of people. Time and time again, I have witnessed people become so absorbed and obsessed with discovering their past lives and conducting the historical research on them that they forget to live for today. At the most, I occasionally read bits and pieces about Lawrence's military career, as that material was most readily available, but when I found myself getting emotionally drawn into his life, I pulled away from it. It made me increasingly uncomfortable. I felt as if my residual feelings toward Lawrence were a betrayal to my present relationship.

Eventually my curiosity about him and what made me love him so much at that time became too difficult to contain. I had one book with his picture in it that was a basic overview of Union commanders and the pages about him had permanent bends and creases because I looked at them whenever I was alone. I couldn't get over how closely the man I had been seeing in my dreams since I was a toddler resembled the man in that picture. The strangeness of seeing him as a sepia image rather than the flesh and blood body I knew was something I could never explain to anyone. The simple things a woman remembers about her husband stuck out the most, like the sensation of his stubble on my face, or his natural scent, or the feeling of his embrace. If past lives were real and I was allowed to come back, then I wanted to know if he came back too.

In October of 2002, I had an opportunity to move back to the St. Louis area. I shared an apartment with my brother and a friend with whom I had gone to high school. I was elated with the chance to have some independence. I did not know many paraplegics or quadriplegics that lived on their own, let alone in an entirely different state from their family. Moving away from home allowed me to become my own person and to finish growing up. I was either going to sink further into a state of depression and anxiety, or I was going to get my head above water and understand that my experiences were my own and I owed no explanation to anyone.

CHAPTER SEVEN

Not long after I moved back to St. Louis, I enrolled in a community college with hopes of attaining a degree that would open the door for a career. My biggest goal was to earn a living for myself and get off of assistance programs like Social Security and Medicaid. Depending on other people or organizations to provide for my survival was something that never sat well with me.

One of the first changes that occurred in me after I moved away from my family was a rather fierce independent streak that would not allow me to ask anyone for help unless it was absolutely necessary. There were countless nights of eating nothing but Ramen soup or macaroni and cheese because that was all I could afford. Along with this new independent streak came the freedom of independent thought. Had I not become seriously ill in the winter of 2003, I believe that I would have come to accept not only the possibility of reincarnation but the reality that I had once lived in the nineteenth century.

On the other hand, if I had not become so seriously ill, I would not have been forced to remain at home for such long periods of time, which allowed me the freedom to explore Lawrence's life a little more. The only reason I continued to ponder the mystery in the seclusion of my own mind was because I was so fascinated by Joshua Lawrence Chamberlain. In many ways, it felt like I was getting to know him all over again. Certain things historians wrote about his personality felt like echoes inside me and I always knew which things were true and which were not, despite not having any formal education in the Civil War.

Winter brought with it what I thought was a run-of-the-mill urinary tract infection but it never seemed to completely heal. The home health company I was using recommended a doctor who made home visits so I would not have to keep going to the emergency room every time I got sick. The doctor went over my complete medical history, and in the process, I admitted that I had been experiencing an unusual amount of anxiety and depression for many, many years. I had seen a television show about people who suffered from panic and anxiety disorders and I discussed with the doctor the possibility that I might have been a person who suffered from the same problem. He agreed and prescribed an antidepressant as well as strongly urging me to seek the help of a counselor or a psychiatrist. I took the medication but I was reluctant to go and talk about my problems with a complete stranger, licensed physician or not. What was I supposed to tell the psychiatrist?

"Hi. My name is Jessica Jewett and I have had dreams and visions of living as another woman in another century since I was a toddler. I don't know how to deal with it. I want it to stop. Can you help?"

There was no way that I would ever feel comfortable talking to a psychiatrist about one of the main causes for my anxiety disorder. I knew that if I ever opened my mouth about reincarnation or ghosts or anything else related to the paranormal, any competent doctor would immediately prescribe enough medication to make me a zombie. My worst fear was being admitted to a psychiatric hospital, which conjured images of darkness, filth and being surrounded by people who talked to themselves.

I was not crazy.

I was not one of those people.

I faithfully took the antidepressant as well as the narcotic painkillers patches that were prescribed for my chronic pain. A year went by in that heavily medicated condition and I no longer felt like myself. I felt like a fragment of my former person, unable to think clearly and wading through a muddy body of water, searching for solid ground. There were times when I tried to carry on conversations with my brother or my roommate and my sentences trailed off into nothing because I could not hold the thought long enough.

The only positive – or so I thought was positive at the time – affect of taking the antidepressant and the narcotic painkillers combined was that the dreams and visions of the Chamberlains stopped. I began doubting whether they were ever real at all. Logic dictated that if medication stopped something unpleasant in your mind or body, then it had to have been some sort of illness as opposed to a paranormal occurrence. My desire to stop the past life from boiling over in to my thoughts blocked any logical sense that I might have been overmedicating myself for the sake of avoiding the emotional pain. True, I was not living with one foot in the past and one foot in the present anymore, but I was not thinking about much else either. I allowed my life to dissolve into a state of disillusionment and apathy. Not thinking about the Chamberlains was achieved, but at what price?

My kidney function began to deteriorate at a shockingly rapid pace and nobody seemed to have any answers or solutions. My urinary-tract infections became so frequent that breaks in between bouts of illness disappeared until I was sick for weeks and months at a time. My doctor ordered a nurse to make home visits twice a week for examinations. She took blood and urine samples once a week at the most frequent and every test came back showing my body fighting off infections that nobody could explain. The doctor routinely prescribed antibiotics until I began to show resistance to those drugs. I lost weight from vomiting every day. I believe that had I not been so medicated on the antidepressant and the narcotic painkillers, I would have had more energy to fight my failing kidneys.

In February, 2003, I spent the days leading up to my twenty-first birthday in the hospital. Being so absorbed in concerns over my health afforded little time to worry about whether the Chamberlains were popping up in my dreams or not. Making the trip to the emergency room for fluids and antibiotics became an oddly comforting routine because at least in the hospital, I was never left alone with my thoughts.

The fevers had begun unleashing dreams from a deeply buried place inside of me and shadowy images of faces from the nineteenth century reappeared. I was so afraid of going through it again that I avoided being left alone. When I did manage to sleep, I did so in the living room several times every week. My bedroom felt too cut off, too isolated and too silent. Silence, I had decided, was bad for me so I did everything possible to keep busy, even when my body was too weak to do much of anything except breathe.

Around that time, I slowly tried to open up to my brother about what I was going through. I expected to be dismissed or told that it was hallucinations because who in their right mind would think about reincarnation as a viable reason? Much to my surprise, he was not judgmental. Naturally analytical and skeptical about everything by nature, he still knew all along that something profound was contributing to my depression and panic attacks. He watched me wake up distracted, sometimes visibly shaken, but it took years for me to be able to open my mouth to him about it. He became my sounding board when I had to talk about things that made no sense and I found that his fresh perspective on the things I saw and felt gave me marginally more confidence than I had felt in years.

After I opened up slightly to Michael, I tested the waters with a friend, Janine, who had experience with paranormal matters. Skeptical, yet understanding like Michael, she encouraged me to investigate Fanny's life and find out for certain if the possibility could be a reality or not. I still felt unwilling to read about Fanny directly but I tested the waters with looking into the rest of the Chamberlain family. The lingering questions from my teens began rising to the surface again about whether other members of that family occupied the bodies of the people in my present life.

One of the first people I came across in my tentative research was Tom Chamberlain, who was Lawrence's youngest brother. The shape of his eyes and eyebrows struck me immediately as someone I was absolutely certain that I knew – both in the nineteenth century and the twenty-first century. Tom Chamberlain, underneath the bushy sideburns and mustache, bore an uncanny resemblance to my own brother, Michael. I knew nothing about Tom on a historical level but as I looked at his photograph, I became certain that I knew him. I presented my brother with the photograph and his reaction was, at first, lukewarm and unconvinced, just as I had been for so many years.

My instincts took over, however, and I started feeling the desire to avidly research the family. The question in my mind developed into quite a black and white thought: how do I prove once and for all that I was or was not Fanny Chamberlain?

Being lost in unexplainable shadowy memories was not going to go away by medicating myself or ignoring it. Like a child tugging at his mother's skirt, the question of whether I was reincarnated or not became harder and harder to push away. I did not have the slightest idea of how to prove or disprove such an idea, so I approached it from a paranormal level instead of a historical level. Once I learned the mechanics of reincarnation itself, if there was even such a guide out there, I thought I could apply those principles to the approach on a historical level.

I read a little bit online, still unwilling to go as far as spending money on a book about a subject that I wasn't even sure I believed to be real. The varying degrees of reincarnation "facts" concerned me because it seemed like people simply wrote things that made sense to them without any authentic facts or research to back them up. As I compared different theories, I saw that a few basics were common among all reincarnation writings.

The explanation of different types of past life memories struck me immediately because it seemed to be the common thread running through even the most outlandish written claims. It appeared that my spontaneous memories triggered by parallel events or familiar people and imagery were common among other people as well. Implied knowledge of the people in the past life without prior exposure to them seemed almost as common, and so did the concept of emotional memories. An emotional memory is a reaction to a trigger by reaction of feeling and unexplained reactions such as sadness or anger from an unknown source. Irrational phobias with no apparent cause, like my phobias of guns, cannons and explosive noises, were thought to be connected to past life trauma.

Stories about other reincarnation cases lacked important details or things that could be fact checked. I realized that a case like mine could be was not very common because most people had no evidence to prove or disprove their claims. Not everybody could accidentally stumble across books about who they had been in a past life in bookstores and not everybody had access to photographs and historical documentation. I had never considered the broader scope of reincarnation beyond whether my case was true or not. It made sense that the majority of people, if reincarnation was to be believed at all, came from masses of undocumented, forgotten people.

The probability that I came from someone of any notoriety when most people had nothing to remind them of their past families except memories made me feel unexpectedly guilty. Why me? What made me different? Why did I have to deal with a past life when I barely had a grip on my present life?

Twinges of resentment took hold in those guilt-ridden moments because I never asked to remember a life that was long gone. I found nothing useful in involuntarily remembering the feeling of holding a baby in my arms when I would never be able to hold a baby in the present as a quadriplegic. I was tired of remembering a man who clearly loved me at one time but could not be found in this life. The whole thing felt like a burden pressing down on me, yet as much as I wanted to turn my back on it, I never really could.

I could not tolerate reading much about reincarnation in one sitting, however. I expected to read about it and find absolutely nothing to validate my experiences. Instead, the pieces of stories I read from other people who went through it were virtually identical to my own, except it seemed that I had experienced quite a bit more than in the average case. Whether reincarnation was real or not, it still did nothing to validate whether I had lived specifically as Fanny Chamberlain in a past life. I endeavored to keep a logical head about it because jumping into something that seemed romantic without being true would hurt me more in the end. I needed to be my own protector because nobody was going to pick up the emotional pieces for me if going on a wild goose chase produced no meaningful outcome.

CHAPTER EIGHT

Fanny Chamberlain made her debut on the silver screen the same month as my twenty-first birthday. *Gods and Generals* was released in February of 2003 as a prequel to 1992's *Gettysburg* – the film that had introduced me to Joshua Lawrence Chamberlain when I was a child.

We were so broke that we had no food in the apartment and we certainly couldn't afford movie tickets. I had only been released from the hospital two weeks before and I was running another fever but I was bound and determined to see the movie. Something told me that despite my skepticism of Hollywood, watching live-action representations of the Chamberlains would, in essence, jog my memory. I also wanted to observe how Michael took in the experience of seeing a representation of his possible former self on film.

I find it amusing that even those who deny their past lives will still have sudden and definite reactions to seeing anything wrong with the portrayal of the period on film. I find it impossible to sit through a film about the nineteenth century without dissecting the accuracy to the point of irritating people around me. The first flicker of the alleged Chamberlain home on screen elicited an immediate, "That's not right," from me. Then as Mira Sorvino came on screen, playing Fanny, an audible gasp of, "Why?" left my lips before I could stop it. While Sorvino is a lovely actress, I disagreed with the decision that she was a suitable casting choice for Fanny. She was blonde, for starters, and the speaking and mannerisms simply were not right.

The major scene depicted between Fanny and Lawrence was supposed to be the moment that she realized he intended to volunteer for the Union Army and leave everything behind at home. I sat in silence in the theater as Jeff Daniels made his way downstairs where Mira Sorvino met him.

"Lawrence, I know," she said.

"How?" he asked.

"I've noticed the way you've been looking into the children's room each night."

At that moment, I drew in a sharp gasp and my face twisted in disbelief. I had no idea where it came from or why so strongly but I felt the oddest urge to stop the film and tell the audience, "This isn't right! This isn't how it happened!" I had to remind myself that to the people sitting in the theater with me, it was just a movie and they had no frame of mind for taking something like that as personally as I did.

During the ride home, I thought about it more and I told Michael that I felt it was wrong. I was not certain of how it happened but it felt like it was on the tip of my tongue. That night I awoke after three a.m., suddenly knowing the answer to the question of what really happened.

There was some sort of paper or document that I had read which said Lawrence had been commissioned into a new regiment. Intense anger flared for a few moments, mixed with betrayal, fear and sorrow, until my eyes adjusted to the darkness and I considered that it was over long ago. Fanny, in my estimation, had not been included in the plans Lawrence made to join the army and it was a source of almost silent bitterness and betrayal for her. She was deeply hurt and disappointed. I could not explain it but I had the impression that Fanny thought of herself as equal or even superior to men, which are feelings which I still have. So when her husband failed to include her in a life-altering decision that affected far more than just his own life, she felt as if she had been knocked down a few pegs. It was a wound from which she did not easily recover.

In the morning, I found a notebook and started writing down everything I knew, stretching back to my earliest experiences as a toddler. I couldn't seem to even enjoy a movie about that period without having an extreme emotional reaction to it and it ignited anger and a passion to get to the bottom of things. I had no idea how to prove or disprove the things I wrote down but I had done impossible things in the past. If I could teach myself to write and draw with my mouth, if I could do well in school despite severe dyslexia, and if I could be a quadriplegic living independent of my parents, then I could certainly find a way to solve the Fanny mystery. Writing was my forte, so I began that way with what I already understood. Just the act of writing it out seemed to soothe my periodic bouts of anxiety over it.

Analyzing my experiences from a logical perspective gave me a sense of order in a highly unorganized and chaotic situation. I felt proactive for the first time in my life where Fanny was concerned and felt a better understanding of why it was happening to me. It was always a lifelong journey, I began to realize, and succumbing to it rather than fighting it was the only way to achieve any peace in my life.

Years later, the first piece of information I wrote down about how Fanny found out about Lawrence's enlistment was validated. I went through a tour of the Chamberlain house in Maine and the tour guide explained that Fanny was kept in the dark about his decision to go. She discovered the truth, it seemed, by reading about it in the newspaper and she was extremely unhappy about it. Had I not written it down, I might not have remembered the circumstances so many years after the fact and had something to compare with what the tour guide said.

Writing became my chief occupation because I was basically homebound as my illnesses continued. Exhaustion became my most prevalent experience and it reached a point of beyond normal fatigue brought on by fevers and infections. I could no longer attend college because of the fatigue and continuous infections. My days became an endless battle to simply stay awake and keep down food. Any progress I had made with coming to terms with the question of accepting Fanny as part of myself or not was put on hold. Still, at night I found marginal comfort in praying, meditating and speaking to those faces I had yet to identify beyond Lawrence. New questions began surfacing in my thoughts. I wanted to know – if I had been reborn, what of Lawrence? Where was he?

The answer came that night in the spring of 2003 when I begged God to take my life and spare me of further pain. I heard Lawrence's voice in the darkness, telling me to fight my illness because there was work for me to do. My initial response was skepticism and to blame the misinterpretation on my own shortcomings as an amateur with paranormal events. A male entity had been in my presence for my entire life but it never occurred to me to try to figure out who he was. Other members of my family had encountered him as well, and no matter where we moved, paranormal activity seemed to follow.

As I looked deeper into the mystery of Fanny, my instinct had always told me from the beginning that I was incarnated into this life without my second half. Lawrence had always been there watching from afar but he was not a living man in this generation. Realizing that I was allowed to know and remember a life in which I was loved unconditionally but I was not going to experience that love this time around was almost more than I could bear. If anything had bred feelings of anger before, they paled in comparison to the thought of remembering him but never being able to know him now. For a short time, it felt as if I was a new widow still trying to get a grip on the loss of a good and faithful husband.

I did not understand why such a thing would happen and I considered the possibility that I was being punished for some bad deed when my name was Fanny. For years I had hated the woman. I hated the way she seemed so cold and unfeeling in any sources where I accidentally read bits about her. I gave in to historical pressure with the idea that she was unworthy of being a wife to such a great and celebrated man. Yet, a few short years later, I had come to a shaky resolution that I had actually been her. Why did I hate her if I *was* her? With little else to go on, I began to believe that I had done something terrible and I hated myself for it – the self-loathing spanning centuries.

My fear that I had somehow caused a lifetime of punishment prompted me, when I was feeling well enough, to explore more online resources on the subject of reincarnation. Unfortunately, a lot of the resources for paranormal topics found online are unchecked, unreliable and provide such varied explanations of the causes and mechanics of the whole thing that a person new to the subject could easily find themselves lost in it.

I read several different explanations for the concept of karma. Some explanations told me that I could, in fact, be repaying some karmic debt by living a life without my other half, while other explanations told me that being reborn, how, to whom, and when is a choice we all make for an assortment of reasons. I had no idea who to believe because I was overlooking one fundamental thought – all answers can be found within yourself if you trust your instincts. I had not learned to trust my instincts.

Throughout the painful ordeal of my kidneys losing function, I had fallen back on old pain management practices that I had learned as a child enduring major surgery after major surgery. The narcotic painkillers were losing their potency, or I was taking too much and building my tolerance too fast, and I realized that I could control my pain level to a certain degree by what one would typically call meditation. I had no word for it *per se*, but I knew how to concentrate on my breathing and relaxation in order to take the edge off of the pain.

To accomplish a state of self-induced relaxation, I laid flat on my back in a silent room with no distractions. I drew in a slow, full breath and let out that slow, full breath while I focused on relaxing each set of muscles in my body from head to toe. Each inhale and exhale followed a time of counting to five. It was a long process that typically lasted a half-hour at minimum. Added benefits to the breathing exercises included the tension falling in my anxiety disorder and the panic attacks seemed less frequent. I taught myself through instinct and practice to enter into that relaxed state without falling asleep because if I found a way to reduce my symptoms, I certainly wanted to be awake for the enjoyment.

One afternoon in the spring, I engaged in my breathing exercise as usual because I had been feeling particularly sick that day. I relaxed far more than I had before, which felt comparable to the semi-conscious state in which a person could partially be asleep but still be completely aware of sounds and activity going on in the surroundings. My thoughts drifted and I rhetorically asked myself, for reasons still unknown to me now, why Fanny never loved Lawrence. At the time, I naïvely thought historians were always right and the general consensus I saw described a woman incapable of love for anything or anyone except herself.

The blackness of my ultra-relaxed state gave way to a dim, muted scene, as if peering through amber glass. Shadows took shape into recognizable figures. A large window covered by white drapes edged in lace. A round table. A chair pulled ajar from it as if someone had just been sitting there. A four-poster bed to the right, though it was not my bed. It was temporary lodging. Lawrence stood between the bed and the table, his knuckles resting on the table, and he wore a uniform that was half-unbuttoned. I felt as tense as he looked and he stood silent with deep worry lines etched in his forehead and fanning from the corners of his eyes. At first, I could not pinpoint Fanny's feelings – my feelings – but in seconds, it became clear. He was going back to fight, and even though I knew it was coming, my heart broke with fear for his life.

I heard myself say to him, "The children need you," but what I had truly wanted to say was, "I need you."

Lawrence's eyes dropped to the floor and after a moment, he reached out and took my hand. The sensation of fleshy warmth, his work roughed skin squeezing my hand stunned me enough that I suddenly woke from the meditative state. My face was wet with tears and I felt so groggy and emotionally wiped out, as if I had literally just endured watching him leave instead of knowing it happened 150 years ago.

I, as Fanny, could not bring myself to expose such vulnerability that I needed him too, even though a person could have knocked me over with a feather in those brief moments of desperation to have him remain with me rather than return to the fighting. As Fanny, I had expressed need and love through the children because something made it entirely too uncomfortable to express it directly.

Perhaps more poignantly, I made the connection that I had asked myself a question in the relaxed state – meditation – and I was able to answer myself, albeit in an utterly draining way. Fanny had indeed loved Lawrence, far more deeply than anybody had given her credit for in present times. Clearly I was misunderstood at that time and I still am. I have been called cold and unfeeling numerous times in my life when the truth is I feel things on such a deep level that I'm afraid people will see my emotions as weaknesses and use them against me.

For the first time, I understood Fanny as an older reflection of who I am today. I began to see the soul as a developing piece of immortality – a piece of clay that could be shaped and reshaped by choices and experiences from life to life. Each life adds new beauty or buffs out flaws if we recognize those flaws. In my case, I no longer wanted to leave the legacy of a cold and unfeeling person when I knew Fanny was never that way and neither was I. The misunderstandings had to stop. Breaking that cycle was one of the purposes for me being allowed to reconnect with my former life. I barely touched the tip of the iceberg in making connections between my past life and my present one. I allowed myself the small possibility that there was a bigger purpose taking shape and I could relieve some of the burden from my shoulders.

Armed with a new piece of Fanny's life, I pulled myself together, wrote it down while it was still fresh in my mind, and I resolved to find a way to prove or disprove its authenticity along with the other nuggets of her life that I had collected. I had to stop being afraid of Fanny and feeling hatred toward her. I had to reassess the situation and look at the possibilities of the parallels and connections having deeper meanings than I ever expected.

Most likely, what I had seen in my meditation took place in the spring of 1864, when Fanny and Lawrence were staying in Washington together before he returned to active duty after serving court-martial duty during the winter.[8] A month after they parted, he was nearly killed at Rives' Salient.

---

[8] Smith, Diane Monroe, *Fanny and Joshua: The Enigmatic Lives of Frances Caroline Adams and Joshua Lawrence Chamberlain*, (Thomas Publications, 1999).

CHAPTER NINE

I believe my early twenties were marked by different points of stepping forward into accepting Fanny as part of my life and then steps backward into rejecting her from my life. Acceptance or rejection seems to have depended on the state of my health. When my health rebounded for brief periods, I felt stronger spiritually as well. After I heard Lawrence's voice in the darkness, I earnestly tried to rally myself, although I picked apart his brief words until I drove myself crazy. What could he have possibly meant by telling me that I had work to do? I was merely trying to live day by day. I had no long-term goals. As I turned it over and over in my mind, I often wondered if I had imagined the whole thing.

May of 2003 brought with it more emergency room trips and lengthy hospital stays. My nurse, who made her twice-weekly visits, found that my blood pressure had bottomed out to a measly 80/50. I could not stay awake and my reaction time was severely delayed. I felt trapped inside of a body that refused to cooperate.

My brother drove me to the hospital and they admitted me right away. I do not remember a great deal from that time because of the lethargy, physical weakness and the ever-present "unspecified bacterial infection" that no doctor had been able to alleviate. Michael remained in the hospital with me day and night, often sleeping in an uncomfortable chair beside my bed. There was talk of moving me to the ICU on the third day after the doctors realized they were not successful in restoring my blood pressure to normal levels.

Discussions with the doctors felt distant, as though I was looking through a tunnel to see something having nothing to do with me, but mildly interesting nonetheless. I felt myself being pulled under a quiet blanket of unconsciousness, which made me wonder how it must feel to drift into a coma, yet sometimes I did not even feel like I was in my own body. Since then, I have read account after account of people having incidences of out of body experiences in times of severe illness, stress or trauma. An out of body experience, sometimes referred to in terms of astral travel or astral projection, entails the soul willfully leaving the body for periods of time to have some spiritual relief. Many believe that the body as a vehicle for the soul is too restrictive and the soul will leave from time to time, mostly while the body sleeps. If my soul ever needed a vacation from the physical, it would have been during those worst days of my illness.

And if Lawrence's presence was truly part of my life – not an imagined thing to explain mysteries – then he would have lingered throughout the illness. As my condition worsened into the third night of my hospital stay, I began talking to someone that my brother could not see. I have almost no recollection of this, except when I woke in mid-sentence three or four times with my brother peering at me as though I had lost my mind. The last time I woke from an unconscious conversation, I opened my eyes expecting to see a nurse standing on the left side of my bed measuring my pulse because I distinctly felt the warmth of another hand on mine. I looked to my left, only to see the vacant space between my bed and the wall. I felt empty, even in such a bad condition, but I did not know why. The familiarity of that hand on mine felt as jarring and needed as the meditative vision I experienced a few weeks before of Fanny telling Lawrence that the children needed him.

Doctors discovered that it was my daily dose of the antidepressant that caused such a bad reaction in my body that my blood pressure bottomed out to almost nothing. As the drug left my system in the following days, my pressure returned to a much safer level and I was allowed to go home. Because I was still weak, however, my mother arrived in St. Louis from Georgia to help in my recovery. The time spent away from her made me realize upon her return exactly how much she could be trusted as a confidante and someone to offer heartfelt advice.

As I watched her vacuum the living room of my apartment, the strongest urge came over me to tell her about what happened in my hospital room. I had never told her anything about the past life questions that I had harbored for years and I did not intend to tell her everything about it. I posed the question of how possible it could be for family members to visit people after they were dead. She told me various stories about my great-grandmother and my grandfather visiting her in dreams and other strange occurrences since they died. That all sounded acceptable to me but I wondered if it was possible for family members from past lives to keep tabs with people presently incarnated.

Who or what determined when we reincarnate and how was it all decided? What was God's role in the process, if there was even a monotheistic god at all? Taking baby steps in seeking my mother's thoughts could not diminish my intense fear that people might find out about Fanny. Although question after question came up in my mind, I could not find the courage to ask them aloud.

In my mind, it was easier to accept the possibility of some kind of spiritual entity keeping company with me than it was to accept the idea that death was merely a gateway leading to multiple lives. Ghosts by their very nature were more socially acceptable. Pop culture had had the power for hundreds of years to romanticize the concept of long dead lovers haunting the living, to horrify audiences with ghouls in the night. But the thought of reincarnation immediately produced the stigma of mental illness or some other delusional behavior. People in general appeared more willing to accept the possibility of a haunted house, person or object than a person believing they had lived in previous centuries. My fear of being discovered almost became a phobia by the summer of 2003. It was safe to accept it in my private thoughts but trying to say it aloud caused feelings of panic and impending disaster.

One or two incidences might be mere coincidence but when event after event adds up over a lifetime, there had to be something more to it. Logic dictated that all things being equal, the simplest explanation had to be true. Exposure to the Chamberlains had not happened in my life until well after I began having spontaneous memories as a toddler. Being so young when it began was proof in itself to me that being influenced by outside sources to create false memories was extremely unlikely. My mother never attended college and had a GED, and absolutely no interest in the nineteenth century, so I knew prior influence could not have come from her. My father was not part of my life long enough to have any influence beyond my lack of trust in men as an adult. The only member of my family who had any interest in the nineteenth century was my mother's oldest brother but we never lived in the same state until I was fifteen-years-old. Any possible influence could not have originated with him either.

I remembered people and events from approximately the age of four that only experts who have studied the Chamberlains for years would have known. If my spontaneous memories had not originated from any outside influence, then where did they originate? The most logical answer to me was that they were my own memories.

The notebook that I had been keeping for the better part of a year filled, little by little, of memories, glimpses of images, people, thoughts and emotions. I kept the notebook up-to-date as best as I could through my illness. I occasionally looked through it but I was not sure of what should be done with it. Keeping a journal and keeping up with written correspondence have never been strong points of my character, which I found out later was something else carried over from Fanny to me.

Instinct guided me more than anything during the spring and summer of 2003 because I simply had no education in reincarnation beyond the scant information I read online. I stopped fighting the possibility that the male entity present in my life was Lawrence. In order to cope with it, I occasionally wrote letters to him that had nowhere to be sent. Writing to him relieved some of the tension I felt and allowed me an outlet to sort through the confused mess of thoughts crowding my brain. It didn't matter if some consciousness left over from his life knew what I was doing. I used it as a therapeutic tool for myself, as people often do when they can no longer talk to loved ones.

Not only did the summer of 2003 bring personal acceptance that I had lived in Maine during the nineteenth century but it brought with it a man to whom I would become engaged. A friend of my brother's, he visited us in June from Milwaukee. I thought very little of him during his first trip to St. Louis other than being my brother's friend but I noticed how much he stared at me. Being stared at was nothing new in my life due to the deformities of my body from my disability and that was how I interpreted his silent attention.

He visited again over the Fourth of July holiday and went with my brother, my roommate and me to a park by the Missouri River for a carnival and fireworks. Again, he lingered around and watched me more than normal. I had gotten out of a six-year relationship only a few months before and the last thing I was looking for was another boyfriend. We talked a little by a small stream off the river and I thought he was nice enough. He told me that he and his family were Civil War reenactors with a cavalry unit in Wisconsin and that was the first moment my interest was piqued.

Looking back on it, falling into a relationship with him was not based on authentic love for him but a feeling of being with someone who understood my eccentricities. Within a few weeks, we drifted into a pattern of talking on a daily basis, mostly about reenacting and the progress on a Civil War novel I was tinkering with at the time. He was somewhat charming and the attention he offered was the kind that I had not felt in a long time. I told him fairly quickly about my past life, and to this day, I'm not certain what made me do that so soon. I hadn't even been able to talk openly about it with my family but I did with this man I hardly knew.

Immediate acceptance from him became an addiction for me. I had lived for years under the pressure of keeping the secret and being starved for acceptance and normality made me rush into a commitment with him and rush into telling him about Fanny. His acceptance and enthusiasm for my situation blinded me to the possibility that it came from his desire to impress me and win me over rather than any genuine belief in it. Even now, I harbor uncertainty about whether he ever honestly believed it or not, but at the time, he provided the role of confidante that I thought I needed.

Despite my lingering questions over his true intentions, I do know that he performed an entirely necessary function in my life. He indirectly planted the seeds in my mind for the process of seeking out parallels and patterns between lives. I learned fairly quickly that his birthday was September 8, which happened to also be the date of Lawrence's birth. That was the first time I realized that there are often patterns from life to life, whether their purpose is for identifying the past life itself or identifying people who were also involved in that life. Common dates, numbers and repetitive names serve as markers of familiarity between lives. Had I never met him, it would have taken me much longer to discover the truth about patterns and parallels.

He was also the person who convinced me that I needed to face my demons in *Fanny and Joshua* that had haunted me since I saw the book four years before. He ordered the book and had it sent to my apartment, saying that I may feel better after I read it and had confirmed the truth for myself. I could not understand my own fears in reading about Fanny. Perhaps it was my deep-rooted dread of finding out that she had done something terrible to justify my life without Lawrence now. Perhaps the weight of knowledge that people never really die forever was too much for my delicate mind to handle. Perhaps it was simply the fear of never knowing real, honest love as Fanny had with Lawrence and their children.

Whatever inspired my reservations prevented me from cracking the book open for weeks. I kept it on my desk next to the computer and never put it away on the bookshelf in my bedroom. Sometimes I studied the cover or read the blurb on the back, underneath the image of Fanny's famous gold, diamond and enamel Maltese cross bracelet, which Lawrence gave her upon the occasion of their tenth wedding anniversary in 1865.

In a fit of ever-present insomnia, I forced myself to open the book and read any page that came to my attention. I looked at it like ripping off a Band-Aid. If I just did it quickly, without thinking about it, the pain would come in a quick burst and then it would be over. I opened the book and read the first paragraph upon which my eye fell. Page 195 read:

> *Now last night after I had gone to bed, Mr Johnson came in with a very distressed manner & begged me not to be angry with him but he saw such grief & ruin impending that he must tell me. Miss Courleander it seems is freely telling people that "you told her (Mrs. Dunning also as well as every body else) that I abused you beyond endurance--pulling your hair, striking, beating & otherwise personally maltreating you, & that you were gathering up every thing you could find against me to sue for a divorce." Mr Johnson says this is doing immense harm, whether the fact is so or not, & the bitter enemies who now assail me on public grounds, will soon get hold of this & will ruin me.*

Snapping the book shut, I sat dumbfounded for an unknown interval of time. What had I just read? It felt as though a brick had settled in my stomach as heavy as the weight of guilt and I wondered to myself if Lawrence was an abusive husband. The allegations had apparently been made in his time but I had never had the contemporary impression that he had ever laid a malicious hand on Fanny or their children. It simply never entered my mind even though it has been suggested by historians that spousal abuse was far more prevalent and far more accepted as the norm in the nineteenth century.

Divorce was extremely difficult for a woman to achieve on grounds of marital cruelty. Most of the time, a woman had to prove beyond a shadow of a doubt that her abuse was putting her life in danger. Even if she succeeded at proving her case, a divorce would have brought shame to both families of the husband and wife, and the two would have been socially disgraced.[9] The theoretical case of the first lady of a state trying to divorce the governor of the state

---

[9] Glenn, Myra C. *Campaigns Against Corporal Punishment*. New York: State University of New York Press, 1984.

would have brought about scandal of such epic proportions that, in speculative terms, Governor Chamberlain probably would not have been reelected. Moving on to the Senate or even the Presidency would never have stood a chance.

Fanny – I – still gathered up a case and seriously considered following through with a divorce despite facing the consequences of ruining the reputation of the family and everyone held dear. Nausea flooded my body as the paragraph replayed itself in my mind. I closed my eyes to steady myself and every part of me spoke clearly that Fanny was not an abused wife. The allegations came from her mouth – my mouth – in a spiteful attempt for attention from a husband who was married to his career.

The only explanation I can find from within for such horrific accusations was a period of feeling so abandoned and excluded that a certain level of desperation arose for attention. Any attention, even anger, was better than none. If he was not going to pay attention to her, then she could elicit sympathy from everyone else. If he was not going to pay attention to her, then she intended to divorce him on whatever grounds she could and go back to her own dreams left unfulfilled when they married.

I found myself breathing heavily, on the verge of a panic attack, suddenly filled with the most powerful regret I had ever experienced. I pushed the book away from me and tears spilled freely from my eyes as if I had just received that letter from him. As I listened to myself repeating, "I'm sorry. I'm sorry," under my breath, I began to believe that Fanny had indeed done something reprehensible for which I was being punished in the present. She accused her husband of beating her in order to try to divorce him. I hated her so much in this life because she hated herself in that life. Even making that connection could not release me from the self-hatred and I refused to read more from the book for several months.

CHAPTER TEN

The end of the summer brought so much change to my life and I welcomed it. I got engaged and moved into a duplex in Milwaukee with my new fiancé and my brother. My mother followed in a few months. Gradually, my health improved in the new environment but I would never fully recover from the beating my body took in the barrage of illnesses over the previous two years. Establishing a life as a soon-to-be married woman took precedence over everything else, although I thought about Fanny on occasion if I saw a blooming red flower or a woman with sad brown eyes.

My fiancé was a blunt, abrupt person. If he didn't like you or something you said or did, he made sure to tell you about it. He established control over the household immediately and most of all, he established control over me. Amidst the power, he continued to show support for my beliefs, my work (I was writing a novel at the time) and he romanticized the idea of me being a stay-at-home wife because he believed I could not contribute to the household with a job due to my disability.

I became, for a time, the pliable and constantly agreeable woman that he wanted me to be because I believed him when he said he knew what was best for me. Our first year together was mostly happy but I chose to ignore the warning signs that I was being psychologically controlled. His explosions of temper were broken by periods of affection and support. I clung to the affection and support while pretending as if the explosions of temper were not happening.

In the winter going into 2004, I came down with bronchitis. Wisconsin was a bitterly cold, snowy place and while it felt somewhat like home to be in that climate, it still felt like I merely existed, waiting for something to change. My fiancé was hardly ever home because he worked such long hours and I had little to occupy myself at home. My false sense of security with him seemed to open the door of interest in picking up the Smith book again. I had a place by the picture window in the living room where I could watch the snow and the similarity to Fanny's Maine home that I saw in Wisconsin winters brought out a terrible sense of homesickness. My reasons for reading the Smith book changed from, "I have to prove myself," to, "I want to read about home."

Quiet calm came over me as my defenses fell and I realized I could simply reconnect with my past for myself. Not for my fiancé. Not for my family. Not for anybody who might speculate and judge in the future. Just me.

Choosing to look into one's past lives will only be a comfortable decision when it's done for the right reasons. Skeptics demand undeniable proof of reincarnation. Not only that but they demand proof of who a person was on a historical level – if the person one claims to have been is not written about on paper somewhere, then he or she must not be real. Or if events one remembers are not written down or somehow historically verifiable, then they must be made up.

Exploring past lives is about figuring out who you are as a soul, where you are headed on your path, and what lessons and relationships you still may need to resolve to advance your path. It is not entertaining the desire to be "somebody." I had no desire for notoriety, nor did I have any desire to explore pieces of the soul. Self-examination is not something a child, or even a teenager, is typically capable of doing, but as I got older, I began having the sense to calm down and look at Fanny in a more practical light. I'm not sure if I was as Transcendentalist as Fanny was but I chuckled to myself with those thoughts of enlightenment through thought, experience and exploration of the self, which were thoroughly Transcendentalist concepts.

In a way, I suppose I wanted to find a way to end the punishment for what I had done in that life by accusing my husband of the worst kinds of abuse. A clear breakdown of the marriage happened somewhere along the line and I felt like I was trying to look at a puzzle with just a few pieces to guide me.

I had a dream not long after I moved to Milwaukee about standing in the old Chamberlain kitchen feeling distressed and barely holding myself together. Another woman stood in the kitchen with me with questioning eyes and it agitated me all the more. I said to her in a quiet, defeated voice, "He will not come home." It was not that I had asked him to come home and he refused. It felt more like I had expected him to come home and be with his family, but when he failed to appear, I felt angry and ignored.

I wanted to know how the situation went from, "He loves me," by the riverbank to, "He will not come home," in the kitchen with that unidentified woman. The possibility that it was my fault unnerved me, especially considering Lawrence's letter in the Smith book. If it was indeed my fault, I needed to find a way to resolve it so I could let go of that life and forgive myself for it.

My exploration of Fanny began in earnest that winter as I was left home to fend for myself most of the time. The first step, I had decided, was to read that little demon book that had been plaguing me since 1999. Once I set my mind to it and began reading, I quickly found that I couldn't put it down. Reading *Fanny and Joshua* gave me the same sensation that a person feels when they thumb through an old family photo album or sift through old family letters. Subconscious thoughts pushed their way to my conscious mind throughout my reading of the book, adding flesh, life and soul to the characters and the text. At times, I sat by the picture window in tears. At other times, I sat by that picture window laughing at Lawrence's teasing sense of humor through heavily quoted letters that Smith used to tell the story. Most of all, I found it comforting to read the actual words of the family again, to hear the echoes of their long-silenced voices in my mind. The little demon book redeemed itself and became one of my most prized possessions.

So much of what I had written in my notebook was validated through reading the book as well. The very first parallel recollection of my father leaving when I was four-years-old coupled with Fanny being adopted at about the same age was one of the first validations that I connected. My horrific nightmare about the wounded man was painfully authenticated as I read the descriptions of Lawrence's wounds, suffering and recovery in 1864. Countless other minuscule and major events, facts and people described in the book helped me to find the same truth just by taking the time to read it. Of course, not everything could be validated. Smith could not possibly recount every minute of the Chamberlain family's life, and neither could any other book, but the amount that I had validated spoke clearly to me that I had touched upon something real. At some point when it moves beyond the probability of coincidence, it becomes something bigger.

Disappointment followed as I looked to other authors for more information about Fanny. I wanted to collect as much as I could so I could compare documented events with the things I had been writing down for the better part of three years. Progress came to a screeching halt, however, when I read how other so-called experts felt about the great Civil War figure's wife. Flighty, cold-hearted, flakey, unfeeling, selfish and vain were the most common words I saw to describe her, if the author even bothered to describe her at all. A few lesser known modern sources went as far as to suggest her coldness toward her husband was due to the fact that she was a lesbian in a time when homosexuality was utterly forbidden.

The way modern authors, opinionates, scholars and the like have thrown daggers at Fanny without sufficient evidence to back up their claims is deeply hurtful to me. I have been forced to toughen up and to remember that it is part of our modern culture to build up the celebrity to a godly status (such as Lawrence becoming a figure in an ivory tower) and then find things or simply make up things to tear down the celebrity. Wading through the assumptions and peering underneath Lawrence's tall shadow to find the truth of who I was has been quite a struggle. Through it all, I have come to rely on Diane Monroe Smith's books as the closest things to truth that I will ever find, short of direct letters and documents penned in Fanny's own hand.

In March of 2004, I underwent surgery to remove three benign breast tumors. Amidst the stress of another medical setback, the tension between my fiancé and my family was beginning to boil over and I felt trapped. His controlling behavior became worse and worse as time passed until he was openly fighting with my brother and my mother. I entertained thoughts of leaving him that spring but I never managed to make myself do it. Now, understanding the patterns of abuse, I know that I had fallen into the routine of, "If I just love him a little more, he will change." I took the blame onto myself for his behavior and when my family moved out of the house, one by one, I was completely isolated with him.

The research into the Chamberlain family became an anchor to keep me grounded throughout my life with my fiancé and although he lost his temper at the drop of a hat, he still supported my exploration. To this day, I honestly don't know why. I would have continued trying to solve the mysteries whether he felt good about it or not. It was one aspect of my life that he could not control and neither could I.

The frequency of spontaneous past life memories seems to be at the heaviest in childhood before a person becomes tainted by social customs. Children do not understand that concepts of ghosts or reincarnation are things frowned upon by society. Children see unfettered truth even though they may not have labels for what they experience. Truth in any form comes with no label or category. Most of my memories made their appearances when I was between four and twelve-years-old, but I also endured sporadic bursts when things in my present life triggered knowledge of similar things from a past life. Months and sometimes years passed in my life with no new pieces of knowledge or remembered events, emotions or thoughts from the nineteenth century.

Underneath the literal memories almost always lies the sense of belonging in a different location or a different time. A person will almost always experience an emotional reaction, positive or negative, to the time periods or world events that they witnessed. In my case, I was extremely pulled to the nineteenth century before I could read, specifically to fashion and matters pertaining to the household, the family and women's affairs. The Civil War was the most significant event in nineteenth century America, so it became the catalyst very early on for me to observe, even though I had no interest in military issues. I almost never read about the battles, weaponry or armies, which was why I managed to avoid explicit coverage of Joshua Lawrence Chamberlain for virtually my entire childhood.

Habits, tastes and the like will also follow people from life to life. While we do live completely different lives with new experiences, circumstances and lessons, the soul is inherently the same throughout. Even if a Caucasian woman incarnates in her next life as an African-American man, the soul within the body will not fluctuate too much from its natural identity. Variations in personality, habit and goals come through circumstances within the life. Despite such variations, the soul will usually revert back to its natural way of being with a new sense of understanding from the intended lesson. Fanny was not abused in her life but I was, which skewed the way I saw the world.

My taste is very similar to what it was as Fanny. As a child, I went to a church in a wealthy St. Louis neighborhood and I always marveled over the fur coats ladies wore. I told my grandmother many times that I should have a fur as well. As an adult, I discovered that Fanny had coats trimmed in fur and people often gossiped about her dressing above her class. Negativity followed her in her sense of style, leading to members of her own family referring to her as vain and her desire for fine things as a weak spot in her character. Fanny's fashion sense was universally described as uniquely her own without a desire on her part to bend to fads or trends. My present life has been marked by similar desires to avoid fads and trends, but to wear things that speak to my individuality.

As she did, I grew up in poverty but felt a sense that I didn't "belong" to that class, which made me find ways to make clothing appear more "higher class". The sense of not "belonging" in poverty was the result of an accumulation of further past life events beyond Fanny and my present life. Before Fanny, I had lived as part of an aristocratic family in France and the habits and tastes from that time carried over into the impoverished future lives. Old habits are exceedingly difficult to break even if one is unaware of the origin of those habits.

CHAPTER ELEVEN

With my family scattered to the winds and I left in isolation with a man less than worthy of my lifetime commitment, I resigned myself to the life I had chosen. I could not break away from the extremely old-fashioned mentality that I could not walk away from a man once promises and commitments were made, so I soldiered on with the engagement despite deep reservations.

We decided to buy our first home that summer and I had an image in my mind of what felt like home – a simple Cape with a decent yard and a fence around the property. He created the illusion that I was involved in the process of house hunting but the truth was I had no choice at all if it was not what he wanted as well. As we toured dump after dump, I grew more uneasy with the odd gingerbread-style houses in Milwaukee.

Eventually, we moved into a small two-bedroom house on the edge of a ghetto. It was a far cry from the simple Cape with a decent yard and a fence that I had dreamed about for years. A strange, yet lucky twist of fate prevented me from being listed on the financial papers associated with our new home and part of me breathed a sigh of relief. Extracting myself, in time, would not be as difficult as I had anticipated. Legally, my fiancé owned the house and I was free to leave whenever I chose.

He deemed decoration women's work, so I was given charge of choosing paint colors for the living room and master bedroom. I never had to give it serious thought. I knew what color to use in the living room before I ever set foot in the local hardware store. I had painted several bedrooms over the years a particular shade of blue that had always given me a warm, homey sensation. It was close to Colonial blue with a little something brighter added to it. When I saw our meager selection of living room furniture, however, I recognized that my blue was going to clash. Determination to have that blue somewhere in my house filled me, though, and I settled on using it for my bedroom, while I chose a muted green for the living room. I had also wanted to paint a room intense red but the house was too small to make it work. Little did I know then just how far back in time my taste in home décor stretched.

As we settled into the new home, I resumed my work in writing a novel that had been my biggest occupation since high school. I developed a circle of friends that served as test readers for me as well. Many of them commented, through the evolution of the manuscript, that my command of the nineteenth century was so adept that it sounded as if I had lived during that time. Of course, I never felt that I could tell them the truth, but their comments ignited a spark of panic. I could not stomach the thought of being found out and the fear made me put away the manuscript on more than one occasion. People stumbling onto the truth that I had been reincarnated from the nineteenth century meant instant lack of credibility as an author and a future historian. In my eyes, it meant my aspiring career would have ended before it began.

Around that time, I saw a television show that, unknown to me then, would change the course of my life. The show featured several paranormal topics every week and in that particular week, a few segments were devoted to the reincarnation case of Jeffrey Keene, a firefighter in Connecticut. Keene believes himself to be the reincarnation of General John Brown Gordon, who served in the Confederate Army. As I watched Keene discuss his experiences and his struggle with logic versus the unseen, I instantly connected with his story. He said at one point, "You can either ignore it or you can look into it," about the struggle with going through experiences that were not socially acceptable. It struck me almost as much as Keene himself struck me with the strange echoing sensation I experienced when I recognized other parallel events, symbols or people from my past life.

Although I was not certain of who General Gordon was, having not studied the Confederacy at any great length, I vaguely remembered the name both from a past life recollection perspective and a vague recollection of reading the name in my research into the Chamberlain family. I looked into my resources and found that General Gordon was born in February of 1832 in Upson County, Georgia. He practiced law before the Civil War and, like Lawrence, took a wife named Fanny, whom he loved dearly.

Also like Lawrence, Gordon entered the Civil War with little to no military education or training, but learned quickly, and rose through the ranks to become one of General Robert E. Lee's most trusted generals. At the battle of Antietam in Maryland, Gordon was shot five times, once in the face, and overcame insurmountable obstacles to recover from his wounds and rejoin his men in combat a month later. Lawrence too endured wounds that should have killed him but his desire to resume leadership of his men pushed him to recover despite all the odds.

I realized, as I read the brief biography of General Gordon, exactly why I had experienced the sensation of déjà vu when watching Jeffrey Keene tell his story. At the famous surrender of the Confederate Army at Appomattox in April of 1865, a formal surrender ceremony was planned. On the Union side, General Ulysses S. Grant, who had given Lawrence a battlefield promotion to Brigadier General less than a year before, chose him to lead the formal acceptance of the surrender. On the Confederate side, General Robert E. Lee chose General Gordon to offer the surrender. The moment of the surrender of the Confederate Army has been the subject of many artists in the 144 years since that day, yet there I realized that I had just seen part of Lawrence's life reach through history and reach through the television like a communication to me from the universe.

Suddenly, I didn't feel so alone. I began reading about Jeffrey Keene on various websites and I studied his case to see if it was indeed anything like mine. Was I as crazy as I thought, or was he suffering the burden of knowledge just as I was? The physical resemblance between Keene and Gordon is undeniable, and it reaches down to residual scars on his body from the wounds he suffered in the Civil War. His handwriting was extremely similar from the past life to the present life, his linguistics was virtually identical, and the parallels of dates, events and people were present, and so on. Keene's reincarnation case quickly proved to me that I was not such an odd creature after all, and perhaps there was indeed substance to my own happenings and experiences.

I wondered how Keene had the courage to not only go on television but write and publish a book telling the world that he is the reincarnation of General John B. Gordon. He allowed himself to go through facial recognition testing by experts and other testing, including a lie detector test, on television and opened himself up to the attacks of skeptics and media alike. In my world at that time, I would rather have died than expose myself in that way.

Once I devoured everything I could about Jeffrey Keene and John Brown Gordon, time pulled me back into old habits. I was not living. I purely existed from day to day, trying to convince myself that everything was fine. My fiancé was gone more than he was home and it was not uncommon for me to be left alone for ten or twelve hours in a day, save a brief lunchtime appearance by a certified attendant. My weight steadily declined and I was not being cared for in an adequate way. It was, for all intents and purposes, years of physical and emotional neglect.

In October of 2005, I began having a couple of dreams. They were a crescendo of a year of occasional dreams about motherhood. The dreams ranged from being about pregnancy all the way through to a boy of about twelve-years-old. Sometimes my dreams were of being in Fanny's body mothering her children, while other times, the dreams were of me in this present life expecting and mothering a child of my own. Early October brought two rather emotionally intense dreams in which a boy of about five-years-old spoke to me and called me Mommy. He said I was not ready to be his mother yet but that he would be back someday. In the background, partially concealed by shadows, Lawrence's figure stood, watching over things.

A day or so after the final dream, I suddenly felt like I had declined into the flu, but when severe abdominal cramping and heavy bleeding began, I knew those were not flu symptoms. By the time my attendant arrived for the midday session of care, she found me lying still, pale, sweating, and clearly quite ill. She asked if I thought I might have been pregnant and I thought it was unlikely because I had been on birth control. She insisted that I call my doctor and he was insistent that I see my gynecologist right away because he felt that it was entirely possible that I was having a miscarriage.

I told my fiancé what was happening and his response was disbelief, refusal to take me to the doctor and to say that I was simply having a severe menstrual cycle. Ten days passed before it was over and I was never taken to the doctor. My attendant did what she could to monitor my condition but legally, her hands were tied and she was not allowed to leave the house with me.

Although my fiancé never believed it, I felt I had miscarried a child as a result of being on birth control and the amount of neglect I endured. The date, I learned later, proved to be an important piece of evidence in my case of reincarnation. When a person goes through events, they do not automatically attribute the dates or events as parallel markers to recognize past lives. As I went through the illness, beginning on October 16, it never crossed my mind that it was a parallel date to more than one of my past lives.

Grace, Fanny and Lawrence's first child, was born on October 16, 1856. In my lifetime before that, the woman whom I worshipped like a goddess, Queen Marie Antoinette, was executed by French revolutionaries on October 16, 1793. In this present life, my brother (who I believe is the reincarnation of Tom Chamberlain, Lawrence's youngest brother) was married on October 16, 2009, without reflection or intention to carry out a major life event on that date.

The phenomena of parallel dates from life to life appears to be an important commonality in identifying past life cases when the cases have enough historical documentation to establish such a precedence. Another reincarnation researcher, Dr. Walter Semkiw, refers to it as the "anniversary phenomenon" and uses it as a standard in a complex research system to establish provable past life cases.

The anniversary phenomenon has occurred in many other cases in my past and present lives. As I mentioned before, my former fiancé and Lawrence both shared a birth date of September 8. In my past life during the Elizabethan period, my life ended on September 8 as well, and my husband at that time was pardoned from execution on October 18, which later became the date of Fanny's death. Years ending in 93 appear to yield significant events for me, such as my execution in 1793, followed by Fanny finally going completely blind in 1893, and my being declared legally blind in 1993. I am, after all, only twenty-seven at this time, and it is fairly certain that further anniversary phenomena will turn up during the course of my life.

In the months that I took to recover emotionally from a bout of illness that was most likely a miscarriage, I thought very little of reincarnation, Fanny or much of anything beyond the miserable state of my life. Family and friends finally caught on to the fact that something was very wrong in my relationship and they began encouraging me to leave. I saw no way out for myself, however, and I fell into depression.

In times when my emotional state deteriorated that much, I felt no desire to think of Fanny because my thoughts inevitably became, "What has knowing about her done for me? Nothing. It's a waste of energy." Unlike others who retreat further into their alleged past lives at unhealthy levels when their present lives become too difficult, I ran away from my past life experiences. If I couldn't cope with my present life, I had no desire to try to make heads or tails of a life that had been dead and buried since Fanny died in 1905.

The following February, a friend told me that something belonging to Fanny Chamberlain was for auction on eBay, thinking I would be interested in it because I had an affinity for the family. As it turned out, the auction was for a letter cover that Fanny had written in the winter of 1862 to her "Cousin Deb." It was the first time I had set eyes upon a piece of Fanny's handwriting in this life and I could hardly believe it. Historical styles and techniques aside, Fanny and I have such similar handwriting that even the unique way I write the letter F is a trait that carried over from that previous life. As I looked at it, I couldn't help but laugh. In elementary school learning to write cursive, my teacher had continually complained to my mother that I was not learning to write very well. The truth was I had been relying on my instincts to write the "old" way rather than write the modern way, which honestly was harder and felt wrong to me. My fiancé looked at the image on the computer screen and even admitted that our writing was strikingly similar.

Although it was just a simple letter cover with no letter inside, I won the auction just after my twenty-fourth birthday and so began my quest to rescue Chamberlain family belongings from being passed around to different antiques dealers. The letter cover was my first acquisition and one of my most unique pieces due to the interesting writing I, as Fanny, had hastily scribbled on it in the last minute. In the top left corner, it read, "send me that paper please with the poem in it, which was sent me from Washington. I left it under my portfolio in the dining room. L. did not send it. it was a Washington paper you remember." In the middle, it was addressed to, "Miss D. G. Folsom. Brunswick, Maine," and in the bottom right corner, it read, "Care of Col. Chamberlain."

Again, I found an unexpected subtle piece of synchronicity when Fanny referred to her husband as "L." Since I began recording my experiences, dreams and visions years before, I had often taken to referring to him in that fashion as well.

Despite my disillusionment with life in general, having a tangible piece of that life and touching an actual object that I had touched more than a century before grounded me in a way that I struggle to describe. I had read a few books, looked at a few websites and talked to a few amateur historians over the years, but the reality of the flesh and blood, the tangible, had eluded me for my entire life. It is not to say that I doubted Fanny existed but as a person who needs to experience things through more than one sense, holding the letter cover from my life in 1862 entwined my life to that life in a way I did not expect.

My desire to go back home to Maine deepened after I had that taste of the reality of my previous life there. I needed to know more than ever if it was completely true. I needed to know if going to Maine would solve my lingering mysteries, breed new ones, make me remember more, or even heal me in such a way that I could completely let go of Fanny and leave that part of myself in the past.

My preconceptions about the paranormal told me that souls hold onto the past because there are unresolved things from their lives. For all intents and purposes, history taught that Fanny lived a full and complete life, although not always happy, so the periodic need to re-establish my connection to that life disagreed with the unresolved business theory. The question of why I was allowed to remember my past increased in potency once again as the Wisconsin winter turned into spring.

The anniversary phenomenon crept back into my life again that April when I made a post on a reincarnation forum online. I had asked the members if they had read the book by Jeffrey Keene and if so, what they thought of it. As it turned out, Keene himself was a member of that forum. My jaw dropped when I saw his name and I became genuinely excited because I knew deep in my bones that this was the one person who could understand and sympathize with my experiences. He wrote to me and said that if I could tell him the meaning behind the next day's date, he would send me a copy of his book since I wanted to read it so much. I thought about it and finally it dawned on me. The next day was the anniversary of the Confederate surrender at Appomattox. It was the anniversary that marked the beginning of the friendship between Lawrence and General Gordon.

The book, *Someone Else's Yesterday*, chronicling Jeffrey Keene's experiences with his reincarnation case arrived in a few days. Once I started reading it, I did not stop except to eat and sleep. I think I read it cover to cover in only two days and when I was finished, I felt like I had been through something as cleansing as the rite of Confession. I wrote to him and told him that so many of the things I had been through were things that he wrote about as well. I left my phone number in case he wanted to talk further about it.

On April 23, my fiancé had the day off from work. That day, I got an unexpected phone call from Jeffrey Keene and afterward, I wrote this entry in my journal:

Today General John Brown Gordon called me up at lunchtime to say hey. He goes by Jeffrey Keene now but if you've read his book, you know what I mean. We have been corresponding by e-mail for a couple of weeks now and I wrote him about my impressions of the book when I finished it. I gave him my number and told him I had a story to tell too and if he wanted to hear it, he could give me a call. Since this man gets stories from scores of people who feel the need to confess to him like a priest, I honestly expected a "thanks, but no thanks" e-mail. Two days later – today – my phone rings with his wife's name on my caller ID.

And then I realized I actually had to tell my reincarnation story to a stranger. Jesus.

My initial thoughts were oh my God, what have I gotten myself into? What if he laughs? What if he thinks I'm mad as a hatter? But Jeff was very kind. The first thing he said was that we share dyslexia in common and then he commented on how I looked just like my ancestor, Sarah Orne Jewett. We talked about a lot of shared experiences and I had three opportunities to tell him who I was before he pushed me to say it. He said, "Let me tell you, I've had people tell me they were Mozart, Crazy Horse, Libby Custer, JEB Stuart, George Pickett...[named others]. So I've heard it all." That sounded like his way of saying, "Quit calling yourself 'that person' and spill your guts." So I spilled my guts. It was hard to say it out loud because it is my most guarded secret, but the more we talked, the more he seemed to understand.

Does he believe me? I don't know. Does it matter? Not really. What matters is he took time out of his life to call me and give me advice about whether I should write my own book on reincarnation. It is a question I have struggled with for a few years. I think the biggest thing holding me back was mistakenly thinking I had to prove it to people. Jeff asks a question in his book, "What would be proof to you?" Not many people, especially skeptics, can answer that because there is no proof. George Washington didn't write in his journal, "I'm going to be reborn as John Doe in 1976." Proof of reincarnation doesn't exist. Evidence exists. There is a big difference. With Jeff's help I have found far more evidence to add to my story than I thought possible and I have just begun my search for real answers.

Am I going to take my story public? I'm not sure yet. My plan is to play with the things I have already written down and see if they take the shape of a book. If my story is meant to be told, it will tell itself. I know now that I don't need to prove myself to people anymore because I know the truth is in me. If my story helps one person realize their own story then my purpose for writing such a book would be fulfilled. In that sense Jeff's purpose for writing his book has been fulfilled as well because he opened my eyes to the best way to see things.

My friendship with Jeffrey Keene since then has deepened to a mutual understanding of what we have individually been through as well as, on my end at least, a cathartic experience with a man who I view as a mentor. The friendship exists in extremely present terms, yet I feel a level of predestined familiarity, suggesting that our meeting the way we did was no accident.

In a certain way, I am comforted by his presence in this life because we both know that he was Lawrence's friend. Lawrence, in my opinion, is not living with this generation but I feel that Keene fills his shoes in some ways by offering guidance and providing the acceptance that few are capable of offering me.

He does not have literal memories of me or Lawrence, nor do I of him, but it does not diminish the friendship between our two families. A person does not have to have literal memories of people identified from past lives to know that those people existed. Often, the sense of, "I feel like I've known you before," is symptomatic of recognition on a soul-to-soul level that is not easily comprehended by the conscious mind.

I began to believe that people incarnate together in groups throughout their many lifetimes. It was a concept that I had vaguely read about before but I had little proof of it in my own reincarnation case. I did, however, believe that my younger brother, Michael, was the reincarnation of Tom Chamberlain. With Jeffrey Keene's entrance into my life in such a serendipitous way, I began to put more stock into the concept of soul groups. General Gordon was extremely important to Lawrence. They did many speaking engagements together after the Civil War, bonded by their mutual desire to heal and unify the country after it had been torn apart for so long. There is an account that when Lawrence heard that Gordon had passed away, he was so devastated that he slumped onto the staircase and wept. Clearly, these men were important enough to each other that it could be indicative that Jeffrey Keene is part of our soul group, or overlaps into our soul group in some way.

Irony or perhaps further synchronicity showed me yet more evidence of the ties between Fanny's life and mine. For almost four years, Fanny relocated to Georgia, having accepted a teaching position at a school for girls in Milledgeville. I, too, relocated to Georgia for almost the same period of time after living in Missouri for most of my life. I made my home in Gordon County and graduated from Gordon Central High School, which were all named after General John Brown Gordon. I had seen the Gordon statue on the state capitol grounds many times before I ever knew about Lawrence, Fanny or General Gordon as people from my previous life.

One thing became clear as the summer of 2006 approached, though. I was grateful for Jeffrey Keene's presence in my life. He nurtured the ounce of courage I had left and his stories as well as his friendship made me want to start coming out of the proverbial closet with the truth that I was once Fanny Chamberlain.

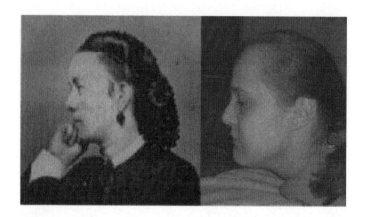

Photo comparisons of Jessica Jewett and Fanny Chamberlain.

Ray Jones, Jessica's grandfather (left) was the reincarnation of
Rev. George Adams, Fanny's adoptive father (right).

Michael Jewett, Jessica's youngest brother (left) is the reincarnation
of Tom Chamberlain, Fanny's brother-in-law (right).

Jeffrey Keene, author of *Someone Else's Yesterday* (left) is the reincarnation of Confederate Gen. John B. Gordon, Chamberlain friend (right).

Bust of Gen. Joshua L. Chamberlain in the Chamberlain Museum.

Two of the thirteen letter covers belonging to the Chamberlains in Jessica Jewett's collection. One is addressed to Mrs. Chamberlain from Joshua L. Chamberlain (top) and the other is addressed to Deborah Folsom from Mrs. Chamberlain (bottom).

Jessica Jewett's childhood sketches of Federal style houses typically found in Maine, despite having never been there.

Another childhood sketch by Jessica Jewett of a house from the late
Victorian period.

A colored pencil piece by Jessica Jewett from 2000 inspired from
Maine winters in her memory.

The Chamberlain home in Brunswick, Maine.

A replica piano and a sofa from the original suite of furniture in the blue parlor of the Chamberlain house.

The Longfellow room in the Chamberlain house (top and bottom).

The collection of Joshua L. Chamberlain's possessions from the Civil War housed in the library of the Chamberlain house.

The library in the Chamberlain house.

Spiral staircase designed by Joshua L. Chamberlain in the red curvy foyer of the Chamberlain house.

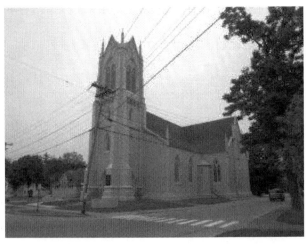

First Parish Congregationalist Church, where the Chamberlains were married in 1855.

CHAPTER TWELVE

The summer of 2006 was both the most difficult and the most life-changing for me. Looking back on it now, I recognize that my probable miscarriage the previous October was the turning point in my attitude toward my relationship. Thoughts of extracting myself from it became louder and more prevalent, especially when my fiancé allowed his brother to move into our spare bedroom. Another person living in your house is the fastest way to bring the problems you have been hiding into sharp focus.

We went to North Carolina to visit my mother early that summer and I chose not to tell her about the miscarriage, about the past life, nor about the worsening of the relationship with my fiancé. In my mind, it was a last-ditch effort to repair the damage and persuade the organism of our relationship to survive. Something that was probably dead long before cannot be brought back to life no matter how far a person tries to run from the problems.

The mountains of North Carolina surprised me in their spiritual energy, their ability to rejuvenate and feel like a refuge for those in pain. I fell in love with it so much that I thought moving there would save my relationship. I have Cherokee heritage, after all, and being so close to the spiritual hub of my ancestors gave me a new source of strength built upon the seeds of strength that my friendship with Jeffrey Keene planted. There, in the small towns, with the foliage, the mountains and the clean air, small rays of happiness began to fill me again. I had forgotten how the simplicity of happiness felt. The happiness, I quietly realized, was not coming from my relationship but from within myself.

When I returned home to Milwaukee, I began putting my toe in the waters of testing the strength of my friendships by telling some people about Fanny. In truth, I expected total disbelief and disdain, but instead, I was met with understanding and acceptance, even if there was skepticism. One of the biggest lessons I have learned from all of this is that skepticism does not always have to translate into hatred. I surprised myself by finding that debates with skeptics challenged my thought processes, my beliefs and my truth in such a way that each of those aspects of my experiences were sharpened and defined.

I also surprised myself in those debates with the knowledge that I could tap into without consciously being aware of it. A discussion about Lawrence's post-war behavior arose among some acquaintances and I could not stop myself from getting involved. Usually I avoided such discussions out of fear of giving myself away but I was starting to make an art form out of debating as an "amateur historian" while taking satisfaction in knowing that I, as Lawrence's former wife, could inject firsthand truth into their discussions. I found that defending Lawrence happened sometimes before I knew I was doing it. More than once, especially in discussing the controversy of our near-divorce, I introduced people to new perspectives.

Lawrence returned home from the Civil War suffering from post-traumatic stress disorder (PTSD). That is my impression looking at it through modern analysis, based on things I remember and have read about from that period. I agree with Diane Monroe Smith's examination that Lawrence had just spent the previous few years in command and accustomed to being immediately obeyed in all things. Returning home to a notoriously stubborn wife and two young children, to a family that had just buried another child, Lawrence could not possibly experience the same obedience to his will that he had in the army. His temper became harsher because, in my opinion, he was not used to being angry at his family and the frustration of no direction in his life was piled on top of things already bothering him.

I know he suffered from combat nightmares as early as 1864. I have a very clear recollection of being woken up because he was thrashing and yelling in his sleep. I believe it was during the period in which we were in Washington in rented rooms. Clearly if he was having nightmares during the war, he would have them for years after the war too.

For some reason, early in my association with such historical discussions, people were reluctant to believe that Lawrence was suffering from PTSD for several years. There is an ivory tower complex about him from some people today that makes it inconceivable to think that he would have such a condition, as if it was a weakness far below him. Ironically, it is basically accepted that Tom Chamberlain suffered greatly with PTSD for the rest of his post-war life and never really rebounded the way Lawrence did.

Amidst testing my own comfort level with allowing others to know about my past as Fanny, I received word that there was discussion in Maine about restoring the master bedroom on the second floor of the Chamberlain Museum, formerly our home. I could not believe I hadn't thought of it before, to try and see if there were pictures of the house in Brunswick, Maine, online. I searched in a few places with no results because, as I had suspected, tour guides did not allow pictures inside the house.

My research into the house showed that it was a one-and-a-half story Cape style structure built on Potter Street in 1825. Henry Wadsworth Longfellow rented rooms in the house with his new wife in the 1830s and hung wallpaper in the front room in 1832 that was replicated in the modern restoration. The Chamberlains also rented rooms in the house as newlyweds and moved to several other rented addresses until finally buying the Potter Street house in 1858. Lawrence had the house moved to Maine Street to face the First Parish Congregationalist Church and Bowdoin College after the Civil War. In the 1870s, the house was lifted and an entire new first floor was built that Lawrence had designed himself, including several oddly shaped curving rooms and a spiral staircase.

The family owned the house until 1939, when the Chamberlains' oldest granddaughter, Rosamond Allen, sold it. For many years, the house was rented out to college students, small families, and so on, until it was all but destroyed and ready to collapse in on itself. In 1983, when I was a baby, the Chamberlain house was saved by the Pejepscot Historical Society from scheduled demolition. Structural restoration took place in the early 1990s and the historical restoration back to the splendor of the 1870s has been slow-going, plagued by funding problems. The upper floors are still split into apartments and rented out to make ends meet rather than restoring the upper floors to their original condition.

The immediate thing I noticed in my initial research into the house was the dates. Fanny was born in 1825, as was the house. The house was saved from demolition in my infancy. It is an unusual parallel, the birth and rebirth of the house coinciding with my birth and rebirth. To outsiders, it might seem strange to be so in tune with inanimate objects like that, but it is virtually impossible to live in a house for approximately forty-seven years without leaving emotional energy ties behind.

I discovered just how strong my emotional ties to that house were when I finally located a person who had been permitted to take pictures on their tour. Each picture had an explanation but I purposefully saved the pictures without the explanations because I wanted to test my residual knowledge of the place. Even though I knew who I was and where I had been, my skeptical streak has never stopped asking questions or demanding more proof out of my own subconscious.

My initial impression was that the structure in the rear of the house that is now the gift shop functioned as a kitchen or some other practical purpose in Fanny's time but I have yet to confirm that. A strong emotional reaction came with photos of the red walled foyer, which Lawrence had designed. I looked at my own kitchen walls in shock, remembering that I had planned to paint them the same shade of red before I decided the room was too small to tolerate such a bold color.

To the right, upon walking through the front door, there was the front parlor and my shock doubled then because the walls in the parlor were almost identical to the blue in my bedroom. It is not a typical blue and I found it unlikely that it would easily be matched by happenstance.

The room to the left, upon entering through the front door, was Lawrence's library, also done in deep red walls with massive bookshelves and a modest but impressive fireplace. His energy presence in that room, even through pictures, is palpable and I had to look away from the images more than once. I had not known there were objects and possessions that survived the auctions and giveaways that Rosamond had done in the 1930s. The pictures revealed the display case in the library that contained several of Lawrence's belongings from the Civil War, including the bullet that almost killed him in 1864. The sight of it, without reading the marker, made me physically sick. One does not need a museum marker to describe the agony Lawrence and the family went through with his near-death experience in the war.

I had never felt a stronger desire to go to Maine as I did that day, setting eyes for the first time in over a hundred years on the rooms that were so familiar to me. Almost all of Fanny's children were born in that house, died in that house, and it was silent witness to illnesses, love, arguing, food preparation, laughter, family, holidays and all other manner of life that left intangible imprints in the walls and furniture. If I was overwhelmed by the tangible connection to Fanny's life from a simple letter cover, then being immersed in the memories and energy of the family home would defy all description.

Around that time, a third person in my soul group was identified, much to my surprise. I had developed a strong connection to a person who admittedly felt that we were experiencing the, "I've known you before," sensation long before I ever told her about Fanny. She knew nothing of the Chamberlain family aside from what she had seen in the film *Gettysburg*, yet she had reactions to Lawrence that would have been expected from Wyllys Chamberlain, the only surviving son. I did not share with her that thought, however, because I knew the human mind was easily suggestible and if my hunch was accurate, I wanted her to find out independently.

Being wrongly influenced is a risk that comes with all who study reincarnation. I have never undergone hypnotic regression, nor have I encouraged many people to do so. The answers about our past lives and the present condition of our souls are inside of us and can be found without the influence of hypnotherapists unintentionally (or sometimes intentionally) suggesting false memories through the regression process. I am spiritually intuitive and I occasionally receive information about people but I do not go to those people and tell them unless they approach me for help first. I do not believe that the study of past lives should be treated as a novelty or a game, so I wait for those to come to me because they will take it more seriously than others.

In the case of my friend, I had a shadowy, hidden feeling that she might have been Wyllys but telling her about that feeling might have inspired false memories. We were close for a few years before I found the ability to tell her in vague terms that I believed in reincarnation and I had many memories of living through the Civil War period. She confessed quite reluctantly that she had recollections of a little boy sitting on a piano bench beside a woman who could play and sing with skill.

Still, I said nothing about Wyllys, although that confession was certainly interesting in my mind. A few days later, I sent her a photograph of Wyllys from his years of attending Bowdoin College. I told her I was not certain of whom it was and I was wondering if she recognized him. Not long after that, she told me in a bit of an agitated message that he looked like her to the point that it emotionally disturbed her. Wyllys was a unique-looking man, so it would not be easy to convincingly say that a person was his spitting image unless the person truly was his spitting image.

Harold Wyllys Chamberlain was born in October of 1858. He was Fanny and Lawrence's second son but the only boy to survive infancy. Another son had been born prematurely a year before and died the day before Thanksgiving, having only lived a few hours after being born. Wyllys did not inherit his father's looks as much as he did his mother's and he also inherited her personality, while the older child, Grace, looked like her father and was, as he described, his soulmate.

Where Grace was confident and set on her life path, Wyllys was insecure, quiet, lost and forever hidden underneath the tall, imposing shadow of his father. He went to law school at Boston University to please Lawrence and had his practice in Ocala, Florida, but his true passion in life was inventing and innovation.

He and his father had a difficult relationship at times. Wyllys never married nor had children, which provokes speculation among historians today that he was a homosexual, but I have never seen any evidence to support that theory. In Lawrence's twilight years, their difficulties diminished and Wyllys became his companion in many ways.

The person who reincarnated from Wyllys has not resolved the things that held him back in that life. Personality traits, habits and coping mechanisms from Wyllys to this life are strikingly similar, and she is too uncomfortable with her identity to come out with it in the way that Jeffrey Keene and I have done. She has rather mixed feelings about that life and the relationships within that life, but, in Wyllys' typical stubborn fashion, she struggles to work through it. She is extremely independent in some ways and needs to do things on her own terms, much like him, yet she seems to have a wandering, lost feeling about her that prevents real success, which was the most prevalent theme in Wyllys' lifetime. She has a family of her own now, which suggests a healing of that part of her soul that prevented her from getting too close to people when she was Wyllys.

The fact that Wyllys has switched genders in order to carry out this life is certainly interesting. In my experience, also corroborated by the research done by Dr. Walter Semkiw, each soul has a dominant gender. Most lifetimes will be carried out as the gender the soul prefers, but approximately 10-20% of the time, the soul will switch genders to gain life experience and learn things from a perspective that could not happen in the dominant gender. I feel that Wyllys is actually a dominantly female soul who chose to attempt life from the male perspective during the lifetime with the Chamberlain family. It is normal and expected for every soul to switch genders from time to time. I believe Wyllys is dominantly female because she appears more emotionally secure and comfortable with her life as a female than the lost, struggling impression that people had and have of Wyllys in history.

Her discomfort with her identity being revealed is also rather typical of reincarnation cases in the Western world. We are continually taught by society that past life memories are concurrent with mental illness, fantasy, and so on. More reincarnation cases are hidden in the shadows rather than brought out to light for fear of ridicule, skepticism and blatant hatred. In her case, the reluctance to come out of the proverbial closet also has a lot to do with unresolved insecurities, pain and confusion from Wyllys' lifetime. If she cannot pinpoint the causes of his pain and how it affects the decisions she makes today, she could hardly be expected to use her case to help others as I have tried to do.

Letting go of old residual pain is the hardest lesson for any person coming to terms with the truth of their past life memories. It's much harder when people suffer from emotional pain that has no apparent cause in the present, yet has causes in the past of which the person might not be aware. Pain travels through time faster than joy and leaves much deeper scars on the soul. A major component in personal exploration of past lives is cutting through the pain, recognizing the causes, confronting them and teaching yourself to let go of things. Residual past life pain can cause irrational phobias and reactions to emotional situations that resonate within the soul as a parallel of something endured in the past.

I have an extremely irrational fear of guns, cannons and every type of explosive noise right down to a popping balloon. As far as I can tell, my extreme fear of guns is a result of watching what Lawrence and other soldiers endured during the Civil War as a result of gunshot wounds. The fear has consumed me for my entire life. I equate the gun with imminent death, even if the gun is only loaded with blanks or not loaded at all, despite my logical mind telling me that it is an irrational fear.

Pain traveling through time faster than joy proved itself repeatedly every time I had nightmares about watching Lawrence suffer in the Annapolis military hospital. Some of the nightmares were too extremely graphic to come from my childlike mind years ago, involving me as Fanny observing nurses or doctors doing painful procedures on him. Other times, I dreamed of a period in his convalescence when infection raged in his body and he became delirious with fever. The agony of him lying there alive but seeing his mind drift away was the most terrifying thing a wife could endure.

Outside of the war, I have had several dreams about Fanny's babies dying and to get to the heart of agony, one only has to bury a child. No deeper pain exists outside of hell. It is not at all uncommon for women who have endured repeated trauma of losing babies to hold onto that trauma and have it manifest in subsequent lives. Losing the first son to a premature birth and two daughters to scarlet fever were things that I felt could have been prevented. Guilt carried over into this life so strongly that I have told people since I was a small child that I intend to have three children "again." The desire to have three children after three children died in that lifetime must be, in my interpretation, my way of trying to have a "do over" so I can fill that maternal void and try to right the wrongs done to my son, Emily and Gertrude.

When old traumas try to manifest in the present life, it is important to face them head-on in order to leave them behind. As I advanced further in studying my past life and reincarnation in general, I began waking up from those nightmares and telling myself specific healing things. I went through months of telling myself things like, "It's over. I don't need to be afraid of this anymore. I'm letting it go. I know who I was but I have to leave the pain behind to allow myself to live freely now. Let me remember happier things. Let me remember joy."

Sometimes the simple act of allowing yourself to feel the fear or sorrow or whatever might be manifesting is all it takes to let it go but sometimes one must be tougher and discipline oneself to let it go. If you do not control your spontaneous memories and the affect they have on your present life, they will control you. Take the lessons and apply them to the present but teach yourself that it is the past and those old things cannot hurt you now.

Adapting the way I thought about my past life memories opened the door for much more pleasant things to come through. Even in the darkest times, I was allowed to feel the glimpses of hope in the old life. Much of it was insignificant, historically speaking, but I have noticed that most people interpret Lawrence as nothing but a soldier, or nothing but a governor, and Fanny as nothing but a soldier's wife, or nothing but first lady of Maine.

The fact that much of what I remember is domestically inclined is not surprising because I was, at that time, focused on Lawrence, children, friends and artistic pursuits. Achievements remembered by history mean very little to me. Medals, ranks, dates and places pale in comparison to the love a mother feels when she sees her child learning new things or her husband telling her she's beautiful when she has been sweating over a stove all afternoon. Do historians care about such things? I doubt it. I gave up on trying to please history a long time ago, partly in thanks to guidance offered by Jeffrey Keene.

One of the loveliest things I remember is a fleeting image of Lawrence sitting cross-legged on the floor in the house with Grace when she was very young. She was about three-years-old and the two of them were engrossed in a book together, both leaning over the pages with the same expression as he read it to her. I used to avoid discussing things of that nature because there is no way to prove they actually happened on a historical level. I have to keep perspective, though, because my reincarnation case is unusual in the amount of historical material that does exist for comparison to my recollections. The majority of people have no documentation at all to prove that their past life memories existed but many are as solid in their truth as I am in mine.

On one hand, yes, historical documentation is helpful. On the other hand, it does not change the reality of a person's past lives. Not every minute of every life could possibly be recorded for posterity, so because I remember things about Lawrence that aren't recorded does not mean they did not happen. The name of the game is not to prove oneself to the skeptics. Going through the process of uncovering past lives, whether it's unintentional or intentional, has to be a personal journey through who you are inside and where you are going on your life path. Skeptics and those who might be cruel about it will always be there and trying to prove a reincarnation case to them will be like spinning tires through mud. It will get you nowhere when you should focus that energy on making sense of why you remember things and how those things affect your soul.

It took me a long time to accept my place in the shadow of a man like Joshua Lawrence Chamberlain. There was a time when I felt a bit of jealousy that I had been reduced to a cameo appearance in most of his biographies. I was not with him during his most glorious and brutal moments in the Civil War and I was a governor's wife with the governor what was at that time hours away in the state capitol. There was and still is no way I could understand the things he did during those years.

Many times, I would tell people about Fanny and they would say, "Who?" I would say, "Joshua Lawrence Chamberlain's wife," and they would say, "Oh, like the guy in *Gettysburg*!"

Yes, with an impatient sigh, like the guy in *Gettysburg*.

I realized, however, that as much as I may be forgotten by history for the most part, I was important to him. The old adage is true. To the world, you may just be one person, but to one person, you may be the world. Whenever I have moments of doubt, I read these words from Lawrence to Fanny written in the early 1850s.

> "...dear the thought just flew over my brain 'How proud I am of her';--for I was holding my pen suspended & I was gazing into vacancy. Yes, Fannie how proud I am of you, and how many hopes I have planted upon you & how tenderly I cherish them believing that one day they will grow up so sweet & beautiful & twine us both, making us one."[10]

[10] Smith, Diane Monroe, *Fanny and Joshua: The Enigmatic Lives of Frances Caroline Adams and Joshua Lawrence Chamberlain*, (Thomas Publications, 1999).

CHAPTER THIRTEEN

I finally extracted myself from my neglectful and harmful engagement at the end of the summer in 2006. It was a situation in which I had to leave rather abruptly. Things turned ugly in the breakup and the courts were involved as if we were getting divorced even though we were not married. The autumn left me in a state of emotional disarray, feeling that I had failed in my life, and failure at anything was not something I tolerated in myself.

I slept in my attendant's apartment for several months because I had nowhere else to go. My life was shattered, I had no money, no home and no possessions beyond my clothes, books and a few other scattered things salvaged from the last few years. Any woman can sympathize with the feelings of worthlessness that came with finding that the man I intended to marry had moved his new girlfriend into my house, into my bed, just a few days after I left. Many of my belongings were still in the house when the new woman moved in and my depression consumed me so much that I went to bed for a weeks upon weeks.

In less than a year, I lost a child, a man I thought I was going to marry, my house, my money and everything that felt familiar. Hitting the lowest point of a life forces a person to reexamine why they exist and what they should contribute to life and the world.

In Fanny's lifetime, she went through the same struggles of self-worth because of expectations that were probably set too high. One thing that carried over from that life to this one was my habit of having such lofty dreams of what love and lifetime partnerships *should* be that the reality of relationships left and leaves me disappointed more often than not. As Fanny, I went through several relationships before I found Lawrence and I fought my attraction to him because it wasn't what people expected. There was no one cheering for us to be together. My father did not like him and his father did not like me. It was quite literal that we were our only supporters because we were set on such different life paths – Lawrence toward a life of service in the ministry and me toward a life of art, music and teaching.

Despite the hardships, the people against us and the differences we had in each other, it was clear even then that we could not be without each other. We were like two trains headed toward each other on the same track. There was nothing that could have stopped us from fulfilling the life that we had planned before we were born into it. I am of the firm belief that we each enter into agreements with other souls in our soul groups to fulfill certain roles in each life in order to teach and learn, to give and take. The major obstacles are pre-planned like tests in school and how we each react to those obstacles determines the success or failure of that lesson or, in the bigger picture, the success or failure of that life.

Lawrence's soul and my soul are what I call twin flames. In the simplest terms possible, most believe that twin flames began their existence as one soul. The soul split into two, became individuals and became like Yin to Yang, plus to minus, male to female (typically, but there are same-sex twin flames).

Twin flames rarely incarnate together but when they do, it is always a romantic connection that serves a greater purpose to humanity. When they incarnate together, it is a lifetime commitment and one will feel completely empty and lost without the other. It is not unlike feeling like your literal other half is missing. When I was first exposed to this concept, it was, without a doubt, the exact impression I felt about Lawrence's soul.

Armed with that theory, I began wondering why I reincarnated into this generation and he did not. Having just left such a terrible relationship, my thoughts turned to a lot of whys about putting myself through such horrible things if we indeed set up these obstacles for ourselves. I went through a period of anger toward his soul because I blamed him for not reincarnating with me in order to prevent the suffering I endured in one form or another for most of my life.

Additionally, my anger shifted to questioning why I was forced to remember the sense of being loved unconditionally when it was clear, at least at that time, that I was not going to experience unconditional love in this life if my twin flame didn't bother to reincarnate with me. It seemed cruel to have those feelings impressed upon me when I could not seem to achieve them again. Mistakenly, I believed that if we had been born together, everything in this life would have been perfect.

As I had a few years before, I returned in the winter to skimming through *Fanny and Joshua* by Diane Monroe Smith, looking for some words, some answer, or some wisdom from the Chamberlains through Smith that I might have missed the first time I read it. What I returned to was the period after the Civil War when Fanny and Lawrence separated and nearly gave up on their marriage. I surprised myself as I looked at the situation through a new perspective as a freshly pseudo-divorced woman.

Lawrence's post-traumatic stress made him terribly difficult to live with – it was true – and I could not understand the darker shades of his post-war character in my nineteenth century mind with no knowledge of the psychological damage inflicted on combat soldiers. Deeper layers, however, revealed themselves to me in a blinding light that made me recognize not only my shortcomings as a woman in that time but that those shortcomings had carried over into this life.

Before Fanny was married, she led an extremely independent life by living in an artist studio in Portland, obtaining a musical education in New York and teaching in Georgia. She was her own person, made her own living and had her own views of the world and the people in it. As an engaged woman, she continued to try to assert that independence by pushing Lawrence to allow her to keep working after they were married in order to supplement his meager income. As I reread those pieces of their discussions, I knew my reasons were only partially about supplemental income but more about an unwillingness to give up my identity to a marriage and to a man.

Throughout Lawrence's successes as a professor and a soldier, I steadfastly supported him (after several arguments about the wisdom of his decisions), but admittedly, I experienced a certain level of jealousy. He was doing wonderful, important things with his life while I was bound to home and hearth.

I was not like many women of that time who were satisfied with that sort of life. I knew there was a bigger world out there and I knew I could contribute to it because I had seen it and I had done it. If I was to be homebound for the most part, I wanted him home as well, perhaps to reassure myself that I was not missing anything by not being at his side. My repeated attempts during the war to join him in camp at the front were because I not only wanted to be with my husband but I felt that I was his equal and worldly enough to be part of this endeavor he was going through. I was not allowed to join him nearly as often as I wanted and members of the family were becoming frustrated that I could leave my children behind for weeks or months at a time. A nineteenth century mother was not supposed to function away from her children.

The real breakdown of the marriage came, in my feeling, when Lawrence became governor of Maine. There was no governor's mansion in Maine until the early twentieth century, so I remained at home in Brunswick with the children while Governor Chamberlain ran the state much further north in Augusta. If he did not seem to need me anymore, then what was I supposed to do with myself besides raise his children? I began carving out friendships with my own circle of people, which gave him fits of anxiety and frustration because not all of them met his standards of goodness and trustworthiness, and in a way, I suppose I did things and chose people to spite him. For a while, the only way to get his attention was to do or say things that he did not appreciate.

Spreading talk of divorce and falsely accusing him of physical abuse was, as I said before, the biggest regret I have from that life but I know now that my intent in divorce was to regain my own identity if he was going to go off and achieve great things. I consider now that allowing myself to endure severe neglect and various forms of abuse in my present life was my way of teaching myself what it *could* have been like and what a mistake it was to do that to Lawrence. Every decision we make has an impact on how we develop as souls and what we might have to endure in future lives.

The attitude I had about giving up my identity to marriage in Fanny's life carried over into this life and I partially sabotaged more than one relationship because of it. As toxic as my former fiancé was to me, the reluctance on my part to adapt to married life cannot go unnoted. Before we were together, I was, once again, living away from my parents in a completely different city on independent terms. I was getting an education at a local college and I had serious goals despite my repeated bouts of kidney related illness. As soon as my fiancé and I began living together, my identity and my independent life disappeared into his identity, his goals and his life. Just as I had with Fanny, I unconsciously found ways to rebel by choosing friends that he didn't approve of and doing things, when I could go out, that he didn't appreciate.

I had blamed many men in my life in the nineteenth century and the men in my present life for disallowing me from being my own person, but the truth was I projected my own self-loathing onto them. In Lawrence's case, as with the man I dated before my former fiancé, they never tried to stifle my identity. Lawrence's desire to be the sole provider was a mixture of being a product of his century and his hope that I would continue to develop my artistry, not for the sake of income but for the sake of cultivating my God-given gifts. Not even my toxic fiancé tried to stop me from writing, art or doing my research. What stopped me then and what stopped me now was my own insecurity and feeling that I was not good enough to contribute anything worthwhile.

Regaining my sense of worth, I realized, was not going to come from the acceptance of a man.

Regaining my self-worth in my life as Fanny was not going to come from divorcing a man that I thought had stifled me and then rejected me for a glorious career in the military and then politics.

I had tried to please men for my entire life and my self-imposed failures left me dejected and contributed to the decisions of allowing poisonous people into my life. Success and happiness could not be handed to me. It had to come from taking charge of myself and how I lived my life. It had to begin by allowing myself the thought that I was worth something in my own right and allowing a man to be part of my life was not necessarily going to threaten my achievements and individuality.

The realizations that come from drawing parallels of such a life-altering nature are precisely why the study of past lives is necessary and should not be ignored. If I had never had spontaneous memory recall from Fanny's life beginning when I was a toddler and if I had not taken the journey of exploring her life in this one, I would never have found the harmful cycle that I impose upon myself.

I remember leaning back on the bed in my attendant's apartment and leaving the open book on the coverlet. I looked out of the window at my side, watching the Wisconsin snow fall, and I felt like a massive weight had been lifted from my shoulders. I had been so angry for months about the path my life had taken but the anger began to thaw as I realized there was a purpose for everything I had been through, both as Fanny and as Jessica. Anger and self-loathing can only come to an end when you take responsibility for your shortcomings, your decisions and the way you handle potentially harmful situations. All of the bad things and anguish we go through are the result of pre-chosen events and are designed to show us deeper reflections of ourselves and the souls around us.

More parallels, connections and theories followed as I sat in silence that snowy afternoon. I considered what possible purpose my disability could have had. If I found myself on the path of letting go of anger toward a neglectful and poisonous relationship, then perhaps there was a way for me to let go of the self-loathing born from quadriplegia.

The question of my disability took a few years to turn over and over in my mind before any theories came to light. My most prevalent theory came through a combination of my research into the wounds Lawrence suffered in June of 1864 and the injury Fanny suffered that led to her death in October of 1905. Lawrence had been shot through the pelvis, which shattered both of his hips, and left him with decades of severe pain, urinary tract and kidney infections, periodic incontinence, and so on. In 1905, Fanny fell at home and broke her hip. She became ill fairly quickly and died two months after the injury, just a few months shy of her 50th wedding anniversary.

I, as Fanny, was not always the most patient person with the debilitating affects of Lawrence's wounds. If the parallel between accusing him of neglect and abuse led to teaching myself about the consequences of neglect and abuse today, then the parallel that I took on symptoms of Lawrence's wounds to learn about what he endured is possible as well. I was born with severe hip dysplasia, which is when the hip joint is so malformed as to appear broken or dislocated and the joints never function properly. I also suffer from chronic urinary tract and kidney infections, and periodic incontinence, just as Lawrence had. If it is true that I chose these symptoms to teach myself more patience and to appreciate what he did for his family all the more, then I have also learned to despise war in any form. War did this to Lawrence. There is no justification, in my mind, for causing suffering on this level to another human being.

My feelings were corroborated by a trance medium reading through Kevin Ryerson in 2007. Ryerson is a well-known medium who has been on several national television shows, published books and worked with actress Shirley MacLaine, who is also an avid believer in reincarnation. I had been put into contact with Dr. Walter Semkiw, who works with Kevin Ryerson in his reincarnation research, and Dr. Semkiw expressed interest in finding out why I was born with such a disability. I gave permission for Dr. Semkiw to ask Ryerson in the trance medium reading about my past life and the reason for my being born this way in this life.

A few days later, Dr. Semkiw called again and told me that Ryerson had confirmed my past life as Fanny Chamberlain, as well as another person's identity from my soul group, and he explained that my disability is a physical manifestation of a protest against war. I have, according to these men, absorbed the suffering men endured in war in this physical form to show that money spent on the military should be devoted to eradicating disease, suffering, starvation and the like from the face of the earth. My feeling about myself in the nineteenth century lends itself to an antiwar stance as well, especially when it came to giving up my husband for another man's cause and watching him nearly die from war wounds.

It is entirely possible that my disability is a physical manifestation of an antiwar protest. It is also entirely possible that I chose symptoms of this disability to mirror the ways Lawrence suffered for decades because I was not as patient as I should have been and I need to learn what he endured from inside the fishbowl. It is clear that there are parallels between my disability and several of my past lives but the specifics of those parallels are not as important as the larger lessons involved.

All of the things I have endured in this life and past lives have had a purpose. Being angry at the circumstances of one's life truly cannot serve the predestined purposes. It's almost like being in school and throwing a tantrum because you are handed an exam. Being angry about life's exams will only derail you for a short time from the inevitability that you will have to complete the exams regardless of how much you fight it.

Love is the correct answer to every exam, whether you're learning by experience and insight to love yourself and accept your shortcomings, or learning to love others despite their shortcomings. Recognizing that those who have wronged you need to be forgiven will free you from the weight of hating them and the things they have done to you.

I forgave my former fiancé a long time ago for the neglect and things that transpired, as well as other men who have inflicted abuse on me, but I have not forgotten, nor will I ever go back to that lifestyle. I have also forgiven Lawrence for allowing me to feel so abandoned during the war and his four terms as governor. Most of all, I have forgiven myself for not being more of a supportive partner to all of the men I have been with, and for not being a better mother, daughter, sister and friend.

I filed away those lessons in the back of my mind and I have taken responsibility for my part in those relationships because I recognized through insight into my past life that I have been going around and around on a destructive cycle of self-loathing and unconscious sabotaging of relationships. The root of destructive behavior, depression and anxiety comes from allowing yourself to get into a position where you cannot find worth or purpose in your existence.

I still feel extremely lonely at times when I receive new information about my former life with Lawrence but I also know that fulfillment has to come from inside of me. Learning about the parallels between my past and present lives has not only confirmed their truth but shown me that, yes, Lawrence's soul is my other half, but his presence – and that of any other person – has to be a bonus to my already fulfilled life. I cannot possibly love someone else and teach someone else properly if I don't love myself.

CHAPTER FOURTEEN

Freedom, after so much time spent being isolated and controlled, was a surprisingly fearful concept for me when I left Milwaukee for the last time in the fall of 2006. There are very few people that a person can fully rely on when things get complicated or difficult but I am lucky enough to have an uncle who has been there since I was born to pull me out of the gutter when I need it. The dissolution of my engagement brought him to Milwaukee to help me through it without question or an accusing eye.

My Uncle Ben took me home to Atlanta with him and I once again found myself a citizen of Georgia as I was when I was a teenager. I lived in the completed basement apartment with my grandmother and I found myself feeling emotionally lost for quite some time. My former fiancé had been making every decision for me as part of his need for control and it ran so deep that I had no idea how to even write a check or open my own bank account. Knowing that I had allowed myself to become one of those empty women one might see on television with no voice of her own because she feared her spouse was more than I could bear. I knew I had been a strong, independent woman once but I felt so beaten down that I was afraid I would never find myself again.

In time, I learned to take control of my life again and remember the goals I had before I got into such a damaging relationship. I began keeping company with people who thought like I did about spirituality, finding strength in spirituality and insight, as well as people involved with Civil War reenacting. I hadn't reenacted since I was a teenager and I always felt an unexplainable level of comfort and consistency when I indulged that part of myself. My desire was not to become Fanny

Chamberlain again. My desire was to use my knowledge of that life to teach the public about a woman largely forgotten by history, aside from the footnote of being the wife of "the guy from *Gettysburg*."

Using the reenacting circuit to teach people was just the beginning of my new take-charge attitude. All of the notes and files that I had collected about my reincarnation case for the past seven years ate away at me. Questioning what I should do with the things I learned went to the forefront of my mind and left me considering the possibility that I had a bigger purpose than I ever thought. If making connections and parallels between different past lives served me like a road map toward improving my weaker qualities and keeping myself from falling into old destructive cycles, then knowing so much about my past lives at all could not be just for my own purposes. To me, it seemed rather selfish and short-sighted to keep the things I had learned just for myself.

The seeds of purpose were planted months before when I began talking to Jeffrey Keene about his experiences, but in truth, neither he nor anyone else could hold my hand through the process. The decision to expose such raw nerves in order to possibly help other people was something I had gone back and forth on for a few years but could never make myself do. I thought it was rather arrogant on my part to spread so-called wisdom to help other people through their lives when I was only in my mid-twenties. How could I have the life experience or the authority to be taken seriously by people twice my age? I knew my story with Fanny was important and I had a bigger purpose with it than the novelty of knowing I went through the nineteenth century but I thought I should have a few more years under my belt before I came out with it. Insecurity still made me fearful at times of being laughed at and ridiculed.

When a person goes through so much trauma, heartache and hardship, however, it is difficult to see themselves from the outside. The advent of social networking websites gave me an anonymous voice in the world and I felt safe talking about my experiences from behind the security blanket of a computer screen. Much to my surprise, my experiences with both this present life and my past life drew people to me. Many of them told me of how much reading my writing helped them cope with their own lives and gave them hope that they could survive the hard times and come out better for it in the end.

Again and again, I was humbled by people who came to me in confidence and confessed that they too had been through spontaneous memories of past lives and that my courage to tell my story made them feel like it was not such a condemnable offense toward society. In the way that Jeffrey Keene had eased my conscience, I appeared to ease the consciences of others just by saying, "This is what happened to me. I don't understand why but I'm trying to learn from it." My young age held no importance to the people who began to depend on me for guidance. In time, my readers numbered in the thousands, many of whom could not come out with their own cases but depended on me to help them through it.

If I had not undergone the adversities in my present life of depression, anxiety, fear, heartbreak and eventual acceptance that past lives were as real as the sun shining on a field of flowers, I would not have been as open to learning or being tolerant and non-judgmental toward other people with their own "crazy" stories. If I had not been forcibly grounded through what is now nearly thirty years of multiple surgeries, therapy and chronic pain to treat my quadriplegia, as well as the influence of bad and good people in my life, I would not have been able to tap into a reservoir of internal strength.

As more people came to me for guidance or just a shoulder to cry on, I realized that things had been falling into place since the day I was born that would allow me to be a voice for those who do not have the strength to come out with their stories. I had been through all that, yet I was afraid of ridicule from people I didn't know. It made no sense anymore. The entire basis of my fear crumbled in that first year that I was away from my former fiancé.

Despite acceptance from friends and strangers alike, I hesitated in telling my family. In fact, much of my family will hear about my reincarnation case for the first time by reading this book. It is not that I purposefully hide it from them. I was never sure how to go about that conversation with people who were a no-

nonsense, practical stock of old-fashioned central Missouri farmers. "By the way, I'm the reincarnation of a general's wife during the Civil War," is hardly appropriate dinner conversation. Every time I thought about it, I imagined the moments of blank stares, somewhat patronizing comments of how interesting it is, and a quick change of subject.

The women in my family have been naturally gifted with psychic, medium, empathic and healing abilities for generations upon generations, but it was never acknowledged. We all have different gifts but teaching each other or bringing it up at all, even though it has always been the elephant in the room, will rarely happen. My maternal grandmother, in her younger years, was an exceptional intuitive with the ability to see spirit entities, receive psychic information and read as well as physically see people's auras. She was always afraid of her abilities and suppressed them, partially because she was trying to raise five children with an alcoholic for a husband. Today, she occasionally still exhibits her abilities with uncanny ease when people least expect it.

One night, I took time to reorganize files on my computer and that included images I had collected from Fanny's lifetime. She walked by just as I had opened a photograph of Lawrence to determine where it should be filed and she stopped in her tracks to look at my computer screen.

"Who is he?" she asked.

Every manner of response flashed through my mind from lying to telling the truth. I told her he was involved with my Civil War activities, which was not a complete lie, but with her failing mind, I was not certain if she could tolerate a discussion about reincarnation.

"He looks sad like he's lost a lot. His eyes are studious. I have the urge to take care of him." She wrapped an arm around herself and squeezed her middle as she spoke.

I casually told her that he had lost a few children and he had been shot, but inside, I ran through past conversations wondering if I had told her any of that in the past. I couldn't think of any instance where I had talked about him or when she might have seen him, except perhaps on the cover of a book. To this day, I'm not sure what provoked her to stop dead in her tracks and talk about Lawrence, whether she was having an intuitive moment or something more.

It is entirely possible that my grandmother is a fourth person in this increasingly intact soul group. She physically resembles Sarah Dupee Brastow Chamberlain, Lawrence's beloved Huguenot mother, and has the same disposition, as well as other parallels such as having five children and raising them on a farm. My grandmother is even a Huguenot as well. Physical resemblance and a couple of parallels are not enough to claim a reincarnation case with any solid certainty, however, and I may never know for sure if Lawrence's mother became my grandmother or not. There is enough evidence for me to keep it in my mind as a theory, a possibility, but it takes more evidence than that to convince me of it as fact.

What is fact, however, is that my grandmother saw spirit apparitions while I was living with her. She had very minimal education in her youth since she was part of the Susie Homemaker generation in which women were bred to be housewives rather than professionals. As a result, she has such a rudimentary understanding of history that she could not identify a Civil War soldier as opposed to a Revolutionary War soldier or a World War I soldier.

One evening, she sat watching television while I was writing nearby, and suddenly she jumped and said that she saw a man walk by the window. My mind jumped to an intruder or a prowler and I said that maybe I should call my uncle at work. She became unusually calm and said matter-of-factly that the man had no legs and was a ghost. I asked her to describe him and the closest thing she could liken him to was, "like Sherlock Holmes but military." I asked her what color he wore and she described it as Confederate butternut without knowing that term. I knew there was a lost Confederate soldier in the wooded area behind the house but I had never told her about it because she had an unfortunate habit of freezing up when anything paranormal came up in conversation.

Later that week, she described seeing another man pass through the kitchen but that man was dressed in a "dark" uniform and looked like he was in better shape than the "man in tan." There is no way to know if who she saw in the dark uniform was Lawrence because she was unable to describe anything in detail, but I never discount any possibilities. I also keep the possibility in mind that her elderly mind may play tricks on her and nothing might have actually been there at all. It is important when researching reincarnation or paranormal topics of any kind to keep a skeptical eye and look out for all possibilities.

A strange side-affect of digging into my past life history through meditation, thought and spontaneous memories came to surface around the time I began helping people through my experiences. Occasionally, I found that I could look at a person on the street or any public place and the present would melt away to reveal who they were in a past life. It seemed that the concentration and focus I spent on my own past had unintentionally opened up the ability in me to see the past in other people. Before I reclaimed my life and my independence, that type of thing would have frightened me and I would have immediately tried to suppress it, but in my new life of being more open and free, I had the attitude that I should just roll with it. Instead of looking at it as a burden or punishment, I looked at it as a new tool in my spiritual toolbox used to help more people find self-acceptance and peace of mind.

I practiced my post-cognitive sight in silence for about a year, testing it out like a new car and figuring out how I might be able to use it. Friends allowed me to use them as guinea pigs and their reactions to how I read them even astounded me. I exhibited the ability to pull together connections and parallels between their past lives and present life in such a way that showed them who they were in a completely new light.

Some began telling me that I needed to take the post-cognitive sight public and make a living off of it since my current income was so meager. I struggled with that for quite a while because I felt that I was a conduit, that information flowed through me from a higher power, and charging money for spiritual guidance seemed wrong. So many psychics I had seen charging hundreds of dollars per hour and using their God-given gifts for profit and then many of those psychics were proven frauds. I knew I was not one of those frauds but I took my gifts – the gift of remembering my past lives as well as the gift of post-cognitive sight – very seriously and in my heart, all of the credit went to God. I felt that I was the funnel through which God poured water.

On the other hand, my quadriplegia prevented me from holding down a normal job. If I had been taught by my grandmother from diapers that God provides no matter what, then it was possible that I was given all of these spiritual tools to not only do good for others but to provide a life for myself too. I had to make the decision of whether I should risk squandering my opportunity for income or risk offending God by using it the way others had tried and failed.

The next summer I went to New England for the first time in this life. I made the flight by myself from Atlanta to Rhode Island in order to spend a week with some friends who work in the paranormal field. I chose not to talk about my post-cognitive sight at all and I avoided the topic of Fanny as much as I could because I simply wanted to be there as a friend enjoying beautiful New England weather, water tubing and tourist attractions. One friend in particular had told me before that he greatly admired Joshua Lawrence Chamberlain but I had never told him who I was. My desire was for us to be friends based on who we were first before I brought the other aspects of my life into it. When I finally did tell him months later, he surprised me with his grace, understanding and support. People like him have somewhat restored my faith in mankind.

Despite my desire to be a "normal" person for a week in Rhode Island, the thought ensconced itself in the back of my mind of how close I was to Maine and Massachusetts, but I was not going to get a chance to fulfill the need to travel there yet. I kept silent for the most part as we drove through the state and across the great white bridge to visit Newport. I do not think Fanny ever spent time in Rhode Island but the scenery of New England, the old Federal architecture, the rocky coast and the inky blue ocean resonated within me. I had never felt so at home in any region of the country as I did there and I knew as much as I wanted to help people, part of myself still needed the healing that came with the validation that the places I had seen in my mind for so long were real.

As I left Rhode Island, I was more resolved than ever that I needed to make a trip "home" to Maine. I had also decided that it was acceptable to make a living from my post-cognitive sight as long as I was fair and responsible about it. Dreams and goals will not simply fall in your lap because you crave them. Blessings only come when you are willing to work for them and take the time to be your own biggest champion and advocate. I knew the gifts I had been given and the experiences I went through were all part of a greater design, a web of paths converging to positive places if I chose.

CHAPTER FIFTEEN

Gettysburg, I have found, is a focal point in the nineteenth century existence for my soul group, as well as so many other overlapping soul groups. Providence, fate or the greater plan at work led me to several other people who had been reincarnated from those who were at or had connections to the Battle of Gettysburg, which took place in early July of 1863.

I encountered several people, who, not knowing my identity, told me stories about having past life memories of serving in the 20th Maine Volunteer Infantry. Long before, I learned not to judge it or be surprised by it if Lawrence's soldiers find their way to me again. Most of the time, I do not feel the need to tell them who I was if I can offer them comfort from more of an anonymous perspective. In many ways, I had learned to be forthright with my former identity when it had a purpose but I never reveal it in situations where it might upset or confuse people even more. Those from Lawrence's old regiment who have found their way to me do not establish lasting relationships. They seem to unburden themselves to me and I have an opportunity to help them understand that they are not crazy, and then for one reason or another, we go our separate ways.

Not every connection from past lives is meant to be lasting. Once we teach and learn what is meant to be passed between us, we let go and move on toward new lessons. Once I have fulfilled everything I need to with Fanny, I will be able to wholly leave that part of myself in the past and move toward new experiences. In some ways, I feel like I have carried the torch of watching over the people that Lawrence watched over in his lifetime.

Quite a few of those reincarnated from the Confederacy have found their way into my life as well. I did not know them directly when I lived in Fanny's body but it seems that those of us who went through the Civil War in any capacity have a quiet understanding of each other. It is not surprising at all that so many Southerners found their way to me, considering that Fanny lived in Georgia for years, and after the war, Lawrence worked tirelessly with John Brown Gordon to help rebuild the South and American unity.

A man from New York contacted me in October of 2007, when I was living with my brother in Tennessee, and told me that he believed himself to be the reincarnation of General George E. Pickett of Pickett's Charge fame. Thoughtful but skeptical, I allowed Paul to call me so we could talk about it further. I am always skeptical of people who claim to be reincarnated from famous historical figures because everybody wants to be the next Cleopatra or Anastasia Romanov or Marie Antoinette. Paul called me the next day and we talked for over an hour about our experiences. He had amassed a considerable amount of evidence over the years, complete with handwriting comparisons, anniversary phenomena, evidence of his intact soul group, and so on. His evidence was quite considerable and my skepticism dissolved the more we got to know each other.

Paul invited me to go to Remembrance Day in Gettysburg the weekend before Thanksgiving. Without hesitation, I knew that I needed to go because I had never been to a place where Lawrence had been in his lifetime. Not only had Lawrence fought the battle there that made him famous and earned him the Congressional Medal of Honor, but he had brought Fanny there to see Little Round Top in the spring of 1864. Going back to Gettysburg, I thought, could be an interesting way to test myself before eventually making the big trip to Maine.

I rounded up a couple of friends at the last minute and we drove to Gettysburg from Tennessee the day before Remembrance Day. As soon as we reached the town after hours of driving, I experienced the same déjà vu sensation that I had many times before where Fanny was concerned. I began telling my friends in the car which buildings were familiar and which were not, and in almost every case, I had picked out buildings that were present in 1864.

The next day, we dressed out in our reenacting gear for the day like all the other reenactors did. My friend brought with her a purple and green silk dress that was original to 1864 and my small stature worked to my advantage for once since I am now the typical size of a woman in the nineteenth century. It was the first time I attended such a large function with people from the reenacting community and seeing the streets of Gettysburg clogged with people in period dress was extremely surreal. The whirlwind of people stopping me to comment on my dress, and that of my friend, led easily into discussions about who I portrayed. Within the Civil War enthusiast community, Joshua Lawrence Chamberlain is the equivalent of a celebrity figure, both loved and hated, so I took my opportunity to educate people about his wife.

One lady in particular was so astounded by my ease with my knowledge of the Chamberlains that she smiled and commented, "It sounds like you know them personally." I knew she was joking and I laughed with her but inside, I panicked a little bit. Civil War reenacting is an opportunity to educate the public in a way that keeps them interested through acting out your parts, but it is by no means based in reality. By that, I mean I was involved in reenacting before I ever knew about Fanny, not because I wanted to *be* Fanny again. I did not want to be found out by other reenactors quite yet because interest or disinterest in my reincarnation case would, in my opinion, detract from the history of Fanny's life and the lives of her family.

That day, I met Jeffrey Keene in person for the first time as well. We met at my hotel and took a walk to a shop where Paul and his wife were selling flowers from her florist shop in New York. Like me, Paul reenacts his past life but I don't think I have ever seen him tell other people about his reincarnation case. Reenacting allows us to teach our histories to people without bringing theology or controversial religious beliefs into it. The amount of Civil War reenactors who are actually reincarnated from soldiers and everyday nineteenth century people is much higher than anybody suspects. It was the bloodiest war in American history and the depth of emotional and psychological scars left on the collective souls who passed through that period appears to make them need to relive it. Some are unconsciously looking for resolution to old problems, others need their sacrifices to be remembered for posterity and others still struggle to let go of the traumas they suffered.

The spiritual energy in the town of Gettysburg as well as the battlefield region outside of the downtown area is filled with the most intense spiritual energy. It is without a doubt the most haunted place I have visited to date with both residual energy and intelligent entities. I went onto the battlefield for the first time that afternoon after the Remembrance Day parade. Keene, my friends and a few others went with me to Little Round Top for support since I did not know what type of reaction I would have, emotional or unemotional. The trek up to Little Round Top on the 20th Maine side is difficult and uncomfortable for those of us who are wheelchair-bound. I had to stop for several breaks before we reached the ground where the 20th Maine fought off the 15th Alabama on July 2, 1863.

Once we got there, I think I went numb for a while. It was difficult to reconcile the two sides of my intuition because on one hand, I could feel the souls still there watching me, but on the other hand, my subconscious mind was struggling to pull out things that I knew as Fanny. Past and present collided in me and for a long time I didn't know how to get a grip and merge the two parts of myself long as we stood in the shadowy woods.

They wedged my wheelchair next to the 20th Maine monument where I would be safe and it occurred to me that I had a photograph on my computer at home of Lawrence and several other people seated around that very spot in the 1880s. His feet had walked that earth. My feet had walked that earth. That land had heard our voices and the din of battle with the cries of dying men from Maine and Alabama alike. I think it was at that moment when it finally hit me that I was really there in a place where I had been with him 143 years before. I had no idea what I should do there except sit and be with the souls of those who never made it home as Lawrence and Tom had. As a woman in those days, I was extremely lucky that most of the men in my existence had come home. They were physically maimed and emotionally scarred but they came home to us. So many never saw home again.

I left Little Round Top that evening with a new, very real appreciation for not only what Lawrence did there but what the rest of the fighting men had done as well. Being so humbled by that rocky patch of earth left me wondering how well I would tolerate going to Maine as soon as I had saved the money to go. It worried me but it was not enough to deter me in those plans. The more validation I had, the more I needed, because I thought it would help me deepen the message of my story.

I attended a ball at the Gettysburg Hotel that night and I met a great deal of people wearing swirls of massive ballgowns, brass, uniforms and performing period dances. By the end of the ball, I felt so at ease immersed in nineteenth century things that it hardly occurred to me that walking about a mile from the town square back to the hotel at two a.m. might have been somewhat dangerous. The streets were dark and deserted with the old buildings jutting up from modern pavement in a strange combination of past and present, just the way I felt in my soul. A particularly old stretch of a street seemed darker than the others and the alleys in between antique houses seemed as silent as a cemetery. We saw the occasional tourist walking along the opposite side of the street but I could not shake the feeling that I was being observed and followed. It was not a negative feeling but it was enough to make the tiny hairs on my arms stand on end.

Just after I voiced the eerie feeling to my two friends, we passed an alley on the right. I looked inside and my eye fell on a shadowy figure crossing from one building to the other, except there were no doors through which the figure could come and go. I felt uncertain about what I had seen and one of my friends declared that it had to have been a tourist, so I passed it off as a trick of the darkness on a living person. We walked to the next block and something else caught my eye on the opposite street corner. I looked closer and realized there was a figure, a black shape of a human, standing at attention on the sidewalk. Nobody with me appeared to notice the figure but as we crossed the street, I could not look away from it. It materialized as a thick mass of black shadow taking the silhouette of a soldier with the faint shape of a red Maltese cross on top of his kepi. The apparition was from the Fifth Corps, which was the corps of the 20th Maine, and I wondered silently to myself if it was one of those boys who had not been able to move on after being killed.

To this day, I cannot say for certain if what I saw was an astounding trick of streetlights and shadows, or if it was a soldier from the Fifth Corps. If it was, had he recognized me or was it coincidence and circumstance of my spiritual sensitivity? So many questions went through my mind that sleepless night that I still have not been able to answer. Whether it was a trick of light or a soldier curious about my presence in Gettysburg, it drove the point home once more of the sacrifices those men made and still make now. Many of them have not been able to move on for one reason or another and they might not even be aware of the passage of time. It is just as possible that my presence stirred something up among the souls still left on Little Round Top who knew me when I was Fanny than it is nothing except coincidence.

I left Gettysburg with hugs and new appreciation for Jeffrey Keene, Paul and all of the people who I met that weekend. The weather froze me to the bone that weekend but the knowledge and validation I gained made the trip well worth my time, money and effort. Increasingly, my confidence in knowing who I was found more solid footing and the thoughts and opinions of those who tried to shut me down truthfully began to lose any power to affect me.

I believe wholeheartedly in the power of thought and the energy put out into the universe through thoughts. I did not always believe in it, just as there was a long stretch of my life in which I did not believe in a breath of reincarnation. A friend who lived in Maine introduced me to the concept of manifesting one's own reality through the power of thought, prayer and meditation. Doing the work toward a goal and going through the motions was not enough. A person must infuse positive thought and energy into the situation and work toward it with the belief that success will be achieved in order to make it happen. Negativity and disbelief would continue to attract negative results in my life if I did not take the steps to alter the way my thoughts flowed.

I was skeptical of that sort of thing because, as with everything else in my life, I need to see the evidence in order to believe it. I trusted my friend enough to believe that she would not lead me into a fool's paradise, so I took the things I had already learned from connections and parallels with my past life and moved a step further by altering the way I thought about my future. Instead of thinking, "I'll never be able to afford a trip to Maine," I began thinking, "I can generate enough work through my post-cognitive spiritual readings to financially support my goals." At that time, my biggest goal, besides completing my first semester of college at home, was to visit Maine. I put conscious effort into removing words such as "can't" and "won't" from my thought processes and pulling myself into believing that there are no goals I cannot achieve.

I put myself out there as an intuitive reader and much to my surprise, people responded. The more I told myself that I could do those things and the more I prayed and meditated for guidance, the more people came to me for help. I balanced solid real-world work in disciplining myself to go through a college education at home with the spiritual work of reincarnation research and doing intuitive readings for other people. I told myself that if it was not working or people were not getting the help they needed from me, I would stop doing that work and do something else. I had no desire to peddle myself as a person with nonexistent intuitive skills as so many others did.

Quite the opposite happened, however. Almost immediately, I received more work than I could handle because it spread by word of mouth about what I could do. I became known as the person to go to about help with coping with past lives, getting started in researching personal cases, and so on. At first, it was unnerving to read feedback from my clients saying the readings I gave them made them cry or resonated in them or directly validated their own spontaneous memories. Inaccurate readings were rare and I found that the further I went into that line of work, the more accurate and detailed I became. I will never forget the times I sent readings to clients and they sent feedback telling me that they found historical evidence of the lives I had read in them. One client in particular actually found the home where she had lived in the nineteenth century and verified the names I had given her through historical record.

Admittedly, doing intuitive readings for people was simply something I did to earn some savings for myself when I first started doing it. As time passed and I saw how much I was helping people, it hit home that I wished I'd had someone to tell me it was all right, that I was not crazy, and to validate my dreams and experiences. I felt that I would never have been so empathetic to those people had I not suffered so much through accepting the truth of my past life. I had not just found a way to earn money. I had found a way to show myself that I could do good in so many ways and serve the higher power through serving the spiritual needs of others. I knew I was a conduit before but it took a while for me to realize that putting out positive energy through intuitive readings was not only healing for me but facilitating positive outcomes for me as well.

Before I knew it, I had enough in my savings to take a road trip in the summer of 2008, a year after I had gone to Rhode Island. I began preparations with two friends to visit Paul and Jeffrey Keene in New York, go on to Maine and take the long way back home to Georgia through Charleston and Savannah. I could hardly stand the wait to allow part of myself to go home again.

While I worked and saved money for my journey to Maine, life threw challenges at my family and me that winter. My uncle found a doctor that was willing to help me with my vision problem. I had been legally blind since 1993 and while my extreme loss of eyesight was another synchronicity with my life as Fanny, I had not been aggressive in seeking help for it. Lawrence had taken her to a few doctors looking for a way to restore her failing sight, to no avail, and my uncle picked up that torch to do the same thing for me. Unlike Lawrence, my uncle was successful in finding a doctor that thought he could help me. I was on the edge of what was treatable and what was not, but I endured two eye surgeries and months of recovery.

At the same time, in Tennessee, my mother and stepfather were finding out that my stepfather was extremely ill. He had been sick since December of 2007 and by April of 2008, the doctors told him that he had pancreatic cancer. It spread before they caught it and as I was preparing for my journey, they told him that he would be lucky to survive until his next birthday the following March. I considered dropping everything and going home to be with my mother but she told me that he wanted everyone to live their lives normally. He was a fiercely stubborn and independent man who did not want people hanging around watching him waste away since he had refused all manner of treatment. They wanted me to go to Maine as I had planned but I knew I needed to go home to them that summer.

A bittersweet air took hold of my preparations for the trip. My family was behind my decision to go but I knew the suffering my mother and stepfather endured made my discoveries a little less important. I felt guilty for fulfilling one of my dreams while my mother's dream of retiring with a man she loved was slipping right through her fingers.

CHAPTER SIXTEEN

For the rest of my life, I will never forget the day I crossed the state line into Maine. We drove through Vermont and New Hampshire to get there from New York and it rained for most of the drive but the weather made no difference to me. I still rolled down the window a little bit to breathe in the Maine air. We stayed in a friend's summer cottage on Little Sebago Lake by the town of Gray. It was beautiful, secluded and offered the kind of peace I needed for reflection at the end of days of exploration. I wanted to see Brunswick and Portland the most, but in truth, simply being in such familiar surroundings felt like cool, healing salve on the wounds in my soul.

The morning I was to go to Brunswick and see the Chamberlain house, the family church and the other sights and sounds familiar to Fanny, I had no conception of what to expect. Would I cry? Would I feel nothing? Would I remember everything? The fear existed deep down in me that my reaction would be akin to the nervous breakdown that Jeffrey Keene endured when he happened upon the area on the Antietam battlefield where he nearly died in his past life. The last thing I wanted was to have a nervous breakdown in front of other tourists and Pejepscot Historical Society employees. How would I explain that without sounding insane?

Drizzly, cool weather welcomed me into Brunswick but as soon as we drove into the older part of town, I knew where I was. An internal compass pointed me in the direction I needed to go if I asked myself where the house was or where the college was or anything else buried in my subconscious. Brunswick, like so many other towns in Maine, is caught between the past and the present.

Strange ironies such as McDonald's inside of beautiful two hundred year old houses or completely modern gas stations between yet more two hundred year old houses are scattered everywhere. For the most part, Brunswick's older historic sections exist just the way they did in Fanny's lifetime and I suspect my internal compass went into overdrive because the visual cues were so present and in my face.

I saw the Congregationalist church on the left side of the street and then instinctively looked to the right and found the Chamberlain house. No amount of mental preparation could have adequately readied me for the sensation of extreme déjà vu coupled with a peculiar sense of tunnel vision. Again, I felt torn between two worlds. I had a new life firmly footed in the present, yet a deep, quiet place inside of me wanted to forget about my quadriplegia and run into the house like I was coming home from an extended trip. Uncontrollable thoughts came to me from time to time, the first being attentive to the fact that the tree in the front yard had grown so much since Fanny's lifetime.

We stood in the parking lot, which was a layer of pavement in the back of the house over part of what was Lawrence's garden, and I looked up at the top floor and compulsively blurted out, "Who put those ugly blue curtains in my house?" All of us stopped, looked at each other and realized that we were going to have to be especially careful about what we said. I took on a private vow that I was going to remain as quiet as I could once I got into the house because I did not want attention or accusing looks from the tour guides. Despite unexplainable verbal impulses, it was no longer my house. It belonged to the Pejepscot Historical Society.

The back of the house is distinctly modern with a carpeted staircase leading up to the apartments as soon as you come through the back door. We missed a tour so we had to wait in the gift shop for quite a while for the next one and I bought quite a lot of merchandise. I'm certain the young lady sitting at the cash register thought we were a little strange because I noticed that she kept stealing looks from the corner of her eye.

Once our turn for the tour came, I remember heading toward the dining room and feeling dizzy and sick to my stomach. Why,

I'm not sure, but as soon as we got into the room, I tuned out the tour guide and went numb. Mentally numb, emotionally numb and physically numb right down to my hands and feet feeling tingly and cold. I was not able to regain my senses until we moved into a back room that was purposefully left unrestored to show tourists what the historical society went through to restore the house from decades of damage by renters.

I felt the first twinges of new emotional impressions of my life there as we moved from the unrestored room to the ruby red foyer, or the curvy room as the grandchildren had called it. The curvy room and the front door in particular left me with impressions of pacing slowly, wandering aimlessly and waiting endlessly, but for what specifically, I couldn't say. The majority of past life memories are not literal images or like movie clips in one's mind. Emotional imprints and implied knowledge from unknown places within are far more common, albeit frustrating with incomplete facts. The emotional imprints are nothing short of experiencing memories with most of the senses numbed.

I was allowed to remain behind while the tour made its way upstairs to the Longfellow room because my friends could not carry me up the winding staircase. As they went upstairs, the irony was not lost on me that the house where I lived in a previous life was probably one of the most wheelchair inaccessible houses in Brunswick. The Longfellow room was the only room open to the public on the second floor and it was the room where Henry Wadsworth Longfellow lived and hung wallpaper as a young man. In the Chamberlains' time, the room was one of the things that made the house so appealing. The tour guide chose that time to talk about Fanny, and in perfect honesty, I did not need to hear it.

The tour leaving me alone with my friends downstairs became a blessing. My numbness wore off and we wandered into Lawrence's library without eyes to watch or judge. The moment I crossed the threshold, it felt like hitting a wall of his domain. My breath caught in my throat and it finally hit me about where I was and the implications of it. Floorboards creaked upstairs with the footsteps of tourists as the most familiar sounds to me and the sense of "home" fell over me in a way that I do not think I have felt in my present life. I have never known what a permanent home feels like or what it is to love a house as part of the family but I understood those concepts from Fanny's perspective as I sat in the library.

Unintelligible fragments of conversations in that room echoed in my mind with the odd affect of listening through a far away tunnel and I experienced historically insignificant but still extremely real visual flashes of things that happened in that room as well. It may have been the sensory overload or the ability to finally let it sink in that I was in the last place that I really felt was home but I lost the stronghold I had on my composure. I cried with the kind of vehemence that made me nauseated and I was not certain of why I reacted that way. I was not unhappy. I was not feeling trauma. I was perfectly happy and grateful to have the experience of being in that house again, yet I sat in the library with tears falling down my face.

As the tour came downstairs again, I quickly pulled myself together and prayed that no one would notice my swollen eyes or red splotchy face. I followed the rest of the tour through the library and into the blue parlor across the foyer. I noticed that one of my friends had broken away from the group for a while and when she rejoined us, she quietly told me in the most serious tone that she had heard boots on the floor in the foyer. She was alone there taking pictures in the library and said that nobody else was there. She was not prone to exaggeration in those things, so I believed her. I cannot say if it was Lawrence or any of the other men who passed through that house over the years but I have always felt especially attached to the style and sound of boots he wore during the Civil War.

We left the house and I wanted to take a walk around Brunswick rather than drive. The family church across the street did not appear to be open but there were workmen there who let us inside for a look around. We waited outside for the workmen to open the door and heard organ music coming from inside, which was such a strange coincidence that my friends all looked at me in disbelief. Fanny had played the organ in the church and worked with Lawrence on the choir for a while rather early in their relationship.

Inside, the great Gothic church impressed me immensely whether it had been my church in another life or not. We found the plaque marking the Chamberlain family pew and I had to chuckle to myself because in my present life in various churches, I had a habit of choosing pews in the same right-hand position of the church. I moved closer to the altar with one of my friends while the other two took pictures of the choir loft in the back. We came to a set of pews on the right side and the vision of young men lined up together there imposed itself over the emptiness.

"The Bowdoin students sat here," I whispered to her.

"You think so?" she whispered back.

I did not think so. I knew so, and she certainly supported me in my experiences. We stopped at the altar where Fanny and Lawrence had been married in 1855 and where Fanny's adoptive father made his ministry career for most of her life. So many significant events happened in that lifetime there for so many residents of Brunswick and the presence of those things seemed to linger in the atmosphere. We talked quietly and one of the people who worked for the church approached us with a friendly smile. He talked to us about the history of the church, where we were from and other things.

Then he paused and gestured to the area where I had just been with my friend. "And the students from Bowdoin were required to attend church here every Sunday," he explained. "They sat over there in those pews."

The validation shocked my friend and me so much that I think someone could have knocked both of us over with a feather but we were careful to conceal any outlandish reaction until he was gone. I knew what I experienced with my life as Fanny was absolutely real but I was not at all accustomed to receiving validation on things I could not have known before I arrived in places where she went. My friend is the type to be rather logical and even tempered. She does not have extreme reactions to things unless they truly deserve it and she appeared shocked for quite some time.

"I knew you were telling the truth," she told me in a hushed voice, "but I have never actually seen something like that happen. You just told me about the college students and then he came and said the exact same thing. I've never seen validation like that before."

Where the house had been Lawrence's and Fanny's domain, the church distinctly felt like Reverend Adams' domain. It felt so different from the house where I had the emotional impressions of a grown woman. The church gave me the emotional impression like that of a young girl wanting nothing more than to sit in her father's lap and hang on his every word. In many ways, visiting the church was more emotional than visiting the house. It touched much deeper, quieter nerves in me and it was unexpected.

Reverend George Adams has already been reborn and died again. Months before I went to Maine, I had an intense dream in which my paternal grandfather, who passed away a year before I identified Fanny, showed me a picture of Reverend Adams that I had seen many times. I did not understand what he meant but I had not seen him in so long that I could not remember what he looked like in detail, so I looked for pictures of him. I placed pictures of my grandfather in a lineup with pictures of Reverend Adams and I realized that I was looking at the same soul in different centuries. I kept murmuring, "Oh my God," over and over again, and stared at the pictures for probably a half hour or more.

My grandfather had a difficult life. His name was Raymond Jones and he married his high school sweetheart, Lou Ellen Pittman, in the late 1940s and went into the Air Force. When my father was three-years-old, a drifter broke into their house for robbery and my grandmother took him by surprise by coming home from shopping. The drifter brutally beat and murdered my grandmother with my toddler father as the only witness and my grandfather discovered her body when he came home that day. My father's testimony sent the killer to the electric chair but neither my father nor my grandfather was ever the same again. My grandfather lost himself in alcohol for the rest of his life, although he remarried a wonderful woman and had another child, a daughter.

Physical resemblance is not enough to claim a reincarnation case, as I have said, but the resemblance added to other parallels and the type of relationship we had, coupled with the increasing emergence of my intact soul group, had led me to believe in the possibility that Reverend Adams became my grandfather. Reverend Adams married young as my grandfather had and adopted Fanny and another daughter. His first wife, Sarah Folsom Adams, died in 1850 and he took a second wife and had a new family with her. His relationship with the family of his first wife was rocky after she died, as it was with my grandfather after my grandmother's death as well.

As a little girl, I remember my grandfather behaving differently with me than other people. He had long since become the strong silent type after my grandmother was killed but he was always more tender toward me. He cared about my development and we had a special connection that, looking back on it now, indicates the "I feel like I've known you before" déjà vu when souls recognize each other. After my parents divorced, I did not see my grandfather anymore and I did not know he passed away until a few years after it happened. It is one of the biggest regrets in my life that I did not get to see him again before he died and that we did not get to share in this journey together.

Had I not been prodded into looking into Reverend Adams by my grandfather, I would not have taken a closer look at Adams' second wife, Helen Root. There was a picture of them seated together that I had seen many times before but I never paid close attention. In the batch of pictures from my father's side of the family that I sifted through to find my grandfather, there were pictures of my stepmother as well. She and I have had a cordial but distant relationship since she married my father, so I overlooked her as a possibility of being part of this soul group. Even as a woman much older than Helen was at the time of her photograph, my stepmother not only exudes the same energy, but looking at my stepmother is like looking at an age-enhanced version of Fanny's stepmother.

If she was Helen, then the dynamics of the relationship have not changed that much. Helen was significantly younger than Reverend Adams and their marriage was not something Fanny accepted easily. The news of the marriage was sprung on her suddenly, as it was for me with my father and stepmother, and there were clear issues of disagreement and resentment between Fanny and Helen. My stepmother and I have drifted even further apart than in that life, if it is her that I have correctly identified. Some relationships are not designed to be close in certain lifetimes no matter if you were extremely close before or not.

I fully credit my grandfather with putting more pieces of my past life puzzle together through the simple act of holding up a picture of Reverend Adams in my dream. Standing in that nearly empty Gothic church filled me with a sense of his energy, the complete father of the past and the grandfather of the present, as if he was there to tell me it was all right to miss him but that he was there watching everything.

CHAPTER SEVENTEEN

A few days after my re-introduction to Brunswick, we returned there to have a look at the Bowdoin College campus. Lawrence went there as a young man to receive an education. He came back a few years later and made a career of teaching every subject except mathematics and sciences. After the war and after four terms as governor, he found his way back there again to become president of the college. Students came and went from his home for the whole of his life and were the heartbeat of that town. Bowdoin gave life to Lawrence and to Brunswick.

At the Hawthorne Longfellow Library on campus, we went to the Special Collections floor to find out if we could see Chamberlain artifacts and papers. The college was filled with people who were obliging and willing to help in any way they could. I saw Lawrence's Congressional Medal of Honor, his glasses with interchangeable tinted and clear lenses, some of his letters, and the "last letter" he wrote to Fanny from Petersburg when he was wounded. We were given access to all of the Chamberlain collection but the vast majority of the letters were photocopies of the originals.

Since we had come from so far, we were given an opportunity to view actual papers and photographs that were not usually available to the public. I was allowed to see the actual letter that Lawrence wrote to Grace during the war when she was too young to be able to read cursive. I also had the chance to see an original tintype of Fanny and I learned that it was made in Jamaica Plain, Massachusetts, where her birth family lived. There were a lot of pictures of Lawrence and other people that I had never seen before.

I read a lot of letters as well. There was one in particular from one of Fanny's sisters, Charlotte, in 1847, before Fanny was with Lawrence, and it was filled with sisterly guidance and teasing about a man Fanny was seeing, only referred to as Mr. Ward. Letters to and from people in past lives usually leave more mysteries than answers. I haven't the slightest idea if Mr. Ward was just a friend or something more to Fanny. It is impossible to know everything about one's past lives just as it is impossible to remember everything from this present life.

Feelings of detachment are normal, especially when the detachment originates with people or events not often seen. People who claim to remember every little detail of a past life or who claim to remember every last person in that life do not seem credible to me. I describe past life memories as being similar to attempting to remember events from one's earliest years. Trying to remember things that happened to me as a toddler is often foggy and open to interpretation. Much of the things we remember from our toddler years are fleeting and make no sense unless someone else or something else like pictures or documents are there to fill in the blanks. Past life memories, whether they are spontaneous or sought through meditation or regression, are much the same way.

After leaving Bowdoin, we walked toward the Pejepscot Historical Society where more copies of Chamberlain letters and pictures were housed. We took a long way around town and as we passed an imposing white home on a street corner a block or so from the Chamberlain house, I froze and said, "That's the Green house." I wasn't sure if I meant the house used to literally be green or if the family who lived there was named Green. I asked my friend if she knew anything about the house since she had been to Brunswick before, but she knew nothing.

"It's the Green house," I restated. "It shouldn't be here, though. I think it had to have been moved like they moved the Chamberlain house."

After what happened in the church, none of my friends questioned the truth of what I alleged. They made comments about how opulent the house looked and we continued on our walk toward the historical society building on Park Row. After I came home from Maine, I stumbled onto the history of that house when I was looking at pictures of old Brunswick. The house was indeed owned by the Green family and the location where I saw it was not where it was originally built. It was moved in 1905, a few months before Fanny died.

"In 1905, the Benjamin Green House in Brunswick was moved from its original location at the corner of Maine and Cumberland Streets to 259 Maine Street. The photograph shows a train blocking the house from moving over the train tracks on Maine Street. The railroad company was afraid the house would damage its tracks. After hours of negotiation, the train finally moved and the house could continue on its journey."[11]

The area of Maine Street and Park Row is still lined with old houses, many of which were the familiar Federal style homes that were there in Fanny's lifetime. In the grassy areas between the two streets, known as the mall, vendors still sold food and crafts and people still picnicked and walked there as they had in Fanny's lifetime. Unexpectedly and suddenly – so suddenly that it cut me off in mid-sentence – I was hit with severe vertigo. I still have no idea why it happened but each time we passed a certain section of Park Row, the vertigo took hold until I felt sick to my stomach and feared being sick right there on the street.

We arrived at the house being used for the historical society and I muttered to my friend's husband, "This used to be a carriage way." A few yards further and a carriage house revealed itself at the end of the narrow path. It had nothing to do with my vertigo that I know of, and I was just beginning to recover from it when we arrived to the Pejepscot Historical Society, but it seemed that when I was distracted by other things, I often commented about how things were "before" without realizing it.

Our time at the historical society was limited, so my friends spread out among the files searching for anything pertaining to Fanny. We found one of her shopping bills from 1856 that amounted to quite a sum of $250 for things like muslin, cotton and several other odds and ends. One thing that stuck out to me in

---

[11] Item no. 9178 of the Maine Memory Network, contributed by the Pejepscot Historical Society.

particular was a letter from Fanny's sister, Anna, who had been adopted into the Adams family not long after Fanny had been. Anna wrote a somewhat dramatic letter that described how a woman named Peabody, I believe, was flirting and carrying on with Lawrence and Anna appeared to think that Fanny ought to do something about it. Anna is another person who I do not literally remember but I have definite impressions of her as somewhat dramatic, meddling at times in the way that Cousin Deb did.

In leaving Brunswick, we drove south down the Harspwell Peninsula to Bailey's Island and Orr's Island. My two friends liked the area and thought it was a good place to see the ocean. Lawrence had a twenty-three bedroom summer home on Simpson's Point, which was on the next peninsula over, but that burned down in 1940. We wandered the shore, picked beach roses and lupines, and enjoyed the sea air. I needed the quiet time to decompress and turn the previous few days over in my mind, to let it all settle in a place inside of myself where I could keep it but not let it confuse my present life. Something comforting and familiar greeted me through the scent of beach roses. On a later trip to Maine, I happened to come across a piece of information through the historical society that Reverend Adams and his second wife had a summer home in that area. Even the smallest twinges of familiarity, as small as the smell of a flower, pointed me toward more truth and more validation.

The next day, we made our trip to the city of Portland. As a young lady in her early twenties, Fanny lived an independent life there in her studio where she kept a circle of artists, musicians and singers as friends. I was unsure of what to expect from the city since most cities held almost no resemblance to their earliest years. Like Brunswick, though, Portland looked like it was in a time capsule fighting against modern progress. As we entered the oldest part of the city by the waterfront, the same internal compass that I felt upon entering Brunswick kicked in but that time, I was not sure of where it took me. I had no knowledge of where Fanny lived in the city, although I had a letter cover from Lawrence to her after they were married addressed to a place on Brackett Street. We found the address but the house was no longer there and the site had become a school playground. It was one of the few disappointing moments, to know that part of my history was erased by progress.

Our real destination was the Maine Historical Society on Congress Street. I had read that most of the written material pertaining to Fanny had ended up there while almost everything pertaining to Lawrence had remained in Brunswick. The historical society library was being renovated but we eventually figured out where things were temporarily stored and I breathed a sigh of relief when library workers did not ask questions about why I wanted to see their Chamberlain collection. They ushered us into a research room and, much to all of our shock, they brought out folders upon folders stuffed with original Chamberlain letters and documents. I thought certainly they would sit and watch us or ask us to wear gloves but they did not and we were left to our own devices.

We sifted through the files for the afternoon and it would take another book entirely to describe the things we read. People have asked me since then how it felt to read all of that and if any of it brought about revelations to me. When a person goes through personal belongings or written thoughts and feelings from a past life, nothing is especially shocking because you have already been through it and the experiences are already stored in your soul even if your conscious mind cannot access it readily. In the sense that a revelation is defined as discovering something new and unknown, the answer is "no." Nothing I found in the documents, letters or pictures were revelations to me since I had already been through it. It felt more like reminiscing in old things that had been temporarily forgotten.

I did find a few surprises in the form of poems. Fanny and Lawrence shared a love of poetry and filed among her correspondence were three hand-written poems that were not signed or dated. It's impossible to say on a historical documentation level who wrote those poems, whether they were copied from something else, whether they were original creations, or when they were written because nothing but the verses themselves remained. My personal feeling on the matter is that two of them were written by Fanny and one was written by Lawrence. The handwriting appeared uncannily similar to theirs when we compared existing documents of known origin with them. The part that haunted me the most was that themes and phrases in those poems were too similar to the themes and phrases in poetry that I had published in this life.

If other things about my experiences seemed impossible but turned out to be true, then I could not discount the possibility that the creative energy put into those poems was Fanny's and Lawrence's and that I had followed the same linguistic patterns in this life. Many other reincarnation cases I had read about showed evidence that handwriting and unique language patterns can remain surprisingly similar from life to life. Whether those poems were original creations or copies of someone else's work, the themes and phrases impressed themselves upon Fanny and Lawrence enough to use time and energy for writing them down. If the poems were not written in their hands but by other people entirely, they somehow found their way into those files of personal correspondence, which shows that they were written by people they knew and the Chamberlains most likely read them at least once.

Emotionally exhausted, I decided we should do something for fun that was unrelated to my research into the Chamberlain family. My friend suggested that we tour the Victoria Mansion because it was something historical that we all liked but she was sure there were no Chamberlain connections to exhaust me further. I agreed to go and we took a walk from the historical society to the mansion.

When we arrived there, the thought crossed my mind that it looked familiar from the street. Then the tour guide said that the mansion was built between 1858 and 1860, so I concluded that Fanny probably saw it on many occasions and admired it. I thought it probably appealed to my "Victorian gaudy taste", as my friend termed it, both then and now. That was enough for me. I simply wanted to be another tourist. We toured the house and when things drew to an end in the kitchen, there were photographs of the Morse and Libby families on the walls. My friend suddenly smiled and pointed to a marker that listed people in one of the photographs. There were Chamberlains in the family. The tour guide heard my friend wonder out loud if they were related to

Joshua Lawrence Chamberlain, to which she replied, "Oh yeah, Joshua Chamberlain's cousin, Arthur Chamberlain, married Mary Libby and the Libby family lived in this house." It seemed that I could not escape the Chamberlain family even when I tried not to be part of it. We had decided at the last minute to tour the mansion for the fun of it but were instead reminded again of why we were there.

On the way back to the cottage on Little Sebago Lake, we detoured out of Portland by way of the last home where Lawrence ever lived. After Fanny died in October of 1905, he tried to carry on in the Brunswick house but a few years later, he closed up that house and headed for Portland. The house he chose was on Ocean Avenue and was a simple white, two-story building, smaller than the Brunswick house. I felt nothing toward that house since it was a place where he lived after I was gone but I did feel sadness knowing he died there in February of 1914. My friend commented that the house was so simple, like he had just given up and bided his time until it was his turn to go. He wrote and worked with the Grand Army of the Republic but even his secretary saw the depth of the sadness in him at the end of his life.

I stayed quiet for the drive back to the cottage. Coming face to face with the last years of Lawrence's life left me reflective in considering his perspective of being the other half of this twin flame match. People can describe the different types of soul-to-soul relationships with emotional detachment but being cognizant of it is another matter altogether. I had lived my entire present life without the physical embodiment of my twin flame nearby but my circumstances now are different than his life as a widower. We had lived together for almost fifty years and then in one day, everything was gone. The passage of time probably felt to him as if it ended in the blink of an eye and feeling the loss of a twin flame often leaves the surviving partner lost. You go on without your other half but you can never seem to fill the void. I don't think, up until that point, I had considered his feeling as though part of himself was missing too.

Considering Lawrence's life as a widower turned my thoughts inevitably to my mother in Tennessee. She sat at home by my stepfather's bedside nursing him through pancreatic cancer that night while we roasted marshmallows on the lake shore in Maine. There was no way to prepare her for life without him, just as there was no way to prepare Lawrence for life without Fanny.

CHAPTER EIGHTEEN

Before I went home to be with my mother while my stepfather went through his battle with cancer, I had heard abstractly over the years that someone preparing to pass away causes the veil between the physical and the spirit worlds to thin. I had never given it much thought because I had never endured the loss of someone so close to me. I had been lucky to not have to go through grief that strong in my life.

We moved into a house in one of the older neighborhoods in Knoxville, Tennessee. It was built in the first years of the twentieth century and it was known as the first house in the city to be wired for electricity. My mother and stepfather had rented the house before he was diagnosed and they had plans to do some restoration work for the landlords. By the time I moved in, he was completely bed-bound and there was half-finished work in the house with tools left there as if everything had stopped abruptly one day. My brother and my friend moved in as well to help my mother get through it.

Living in a home with someone who is terminally ill is like living in the eye of a hurricane. The world outside of your doorstep goes on in its fast-paced nonchalant way, completely unaware of the still and quiet inside of your home. Stepping inside of the home was like pressing the slow motion button and entering a bubble of silence. We all knew what was happening but we avoided calling it what it was most of the time. Then there were moments of profound clarity in which talking about it as a fact of life overtook the waiting and silence. None of us wanted to admit that he was dying, although my mother seemed to have moments of transparency that were straightforwardly moments of quiet rage.

I shifted my thinking from myself to how best I could serve my family. I continued doing my intuitive readings but I poured almost every penny I earned into paying bills, buying groceries and trying to get my mother out of the house once in a while. Her devotion to my stepfather's care was absolute but she was not taking care of herself. My brother, my friend and I took it upon ourselves to take care of her so she could be more mentally and emotionally equipped to care for my stepfather.

Almost immediately after I moved into the house, we all noticed that the connection to the spirit world seemed to be plugged directly into where we lived. I lived on the bottom floor in a room near the staircase and nearly every night, I witnessed a silhouette of a person sitting on the steps. It became a pattern of mine to roll over and turn my back to it so I could sleep but almost every night, I was woken again by the sound of boots pacing my hardwood bedroom floors. It was the same sound I had heard many times in my life, a sound that I attributed to Lawrence's army boots, but not even he could save my family from the trauma.

My stepfather, in his lucid moments before and after the cancer really took a stranglehold, talked candidly about his parents coming to talk to him. His parents had both passed away when he was a teenager. He described instances when he was beginning to see the light a few months before he died and the fear with which he coped. He knew there was an afterlife and he knew the house was filled with spirits ready to help him and us endure his transition from life to death, but he feared the unknown. More than that, he feared leaving my mother alone when he considered it his responsibility to provide for her. Theirs was an equal partnership in a lot of ways but they also had roles of provider and dependent, in a mix of progress and tradition much the way Lawrence and Fanny had in their life together.

I think I would have possibly doubted my stepfather's talk about spirits talking to him in the house if no one else experienced anything. Medication, painkillers and just the process of the body dying can lead to hallucinations and a skewed perception of reality. The reality, however, was that we all experienced multiple encounters with spirits ourselves. I realized that he was giving us truth directly from those on the other side of the veil when he began talking about reincarnation with my mother. Part of her struggle was trying to accept why they only had about five years together when she felt that they were destined for one another. He explained things from a reincarnation perspective in a way I found astonishing because he described things that my mother and I had both dreamed about in years past but never told him. I cannot recall ever having a discussion about reincarnation with him because he lived his life walking the line of believer and skeptic.

The further the summer went on, the more we experienced of those whom we called "the houseguests." One afternoon, we were all downstairs in my bedroom while my stepfather was asleep. My mother started to go back upstairs to check on him and suddenly the sound of rapid pounding feet on the floor above made all of us jump. It sounded like a small child running across the floor in my friend's bedroom, which was directly above mine. The women living in my household all had one thing in common – we had all lost a child at some point in our lives. The three of us were taken aback by it for quite a while and we never truly resolved whether the children we lost could have been part of "the houseguests" or not.

Despite the horrific waiting game we played, a routine fell in to place and I continued doing intuitive readings, writing and putting together the pieces of my past lives. The daily routine slowed my mind enough to be able to absorb my experiences in Maine two months after I returned home. I felt a sense of completion that had eluded me for my entire life where the past was concerned and the merciful peace of uninterrupted sleep became a luxury I hadn't felt before. It was not that I had dreams every night about it but there were times when dreams became so intense that they interrupted sleep and affected how well I functioned in my daily life. The simple act of going back to Maine, confronting the tangible pieces of that life, and turning it into positive work for others, channeled my anxiety into things that pulled me away from the dreams. For a long time after going to Maine, sleep was a blessed, calming activity rather than something I had learned to dread in my life.

Whenever I saved any extra money, I collected the Chamberlain papers from online auctions whenever I could afford them. The thought of those things being passed around endlessly to different antiques dealers bothered me and I decided that even if I had no earthly attachment to them now, at least I could save them from possible destruction. I collected several letter covers written by different members of the family, friends and colleagues. I acquired a certificate issued to a Maine soldier while Lawrence was governor, as well as various books from that lifetime, and so on.

One of the most important pieces in my collection came from Fanny's birth mother – a letter written to Fanny after she had gone back to Massachusetts for the first time since her adoption. Fanny was in her early adolescence and the letter offered rare insight into glimpses of her personality and the world of her birth family.

Jamaica Plain, Dec. 14th, 1838

Day after day passes, my dear Frances; we think of you and talk of you, have hoped to hear before this, of your safe arrival at home, & all that has occurred there, most interesting to you. I was much disappointed in not seeing you on the afternoon of the day that you left us. I had been...troubled with the tooth ache, and made an appointment that morning to get cured if I could, and as it was a busy morning with us, I left you, and expected to pass two or three quiet hours with you at the Marlborough House, whither I went, at an early hour, but I waited in vain, until five o'clock, watching every person that came in. It was a place where I had never been, but there was a nice quiet sitting room, and all things comfortable. I at length took my solitary way homewards, disconsolate, & in the dark, found all had returned some time before, and were wondering where I was. You may laugh a little at my expense.

What a change is there as I look from the window, since you were here. Winter has come. The leafless trees, and fields stripped of their verdure, look desolate & dreary; our weekly walk is still more tedious when the wind blows bleak & chill, but as the fire burns bright and clear, and we are snugly seated beside it, we do not heed the cheerless scene without. Here sits Aunt Dexter, who is making the long promised visit. Catherine, Mary and Charlotte, plying their needles and calling forth their choicest ingenuity in making some article for a fair which is getting up in Mr. Abbot's Society. The object is to assist in procuring a bell for his Meeting House.

Our family remain much the same with the addition of one new boy. Mr. Lacont has absented himself for several weeks, but within a day or two, has suddenly presented his image again to us. Mrs. Evans, an important personage in our establishment, also has taken a french leave & we have not set our eyes upon her as yet.

Our music has almost ceased, but at times some air which you used to practice, is played, and it brings you, my dear child, fresh to our minds. You are now engaged, I dare say, in some useful studies. Now is the precious time; it will be harder to learn by & by. You must try to cultivate a taste for reading - the works of good authors selected and attentively perused, tend much to improve and strengthen the mind. How I should like to have you begin a little journal, and employ a few moments once or twice a week, in writing to me, Mary or Charlotte. Write without effort, or study, and familiarly tell us the occurrences of the day or moment. Give us your thoughts with freedom, all will interest us, coming from you. Perhaps in this way, you would learn to love writing - early familiar exercises of this kind are very improving. I hope my dear, you will at least give an answer to this soon, for I wish much, and we all do, to hear from you, how you got home, whether your health continues good, who you saw first, & how your dear friends all are, what you are learning at school, &c. Do you play much now? What is your father's favourite air?

Adieu my dear child...Be good & be happy, is the wish of your affectionate Mother, E. Adams.

Finding that letter came at the most serendipitous time. About two or three weeks before, a woman named Rebecca came to me unexpectedly and questioned me about the circumstances of Fanny's adoption. She explained feeling the sense of loss for most of her life that women often feel when they have to give up one of their children, even though she had a full and complete family of her own. I had never encountered that type of situation in which a person came to me with possible memories and connections to one of my past lives so I was not sure how to handle it. I knew that I could not handle the case myself because it was too close to me personally and it would be too difficult to keep my judgment unclouded.

I sent her to someone who I worked with on intuitive readings and reincarnation research. A long week passed before we received word about the possibility of who she was, if anyone. My colleague told us things she picked up about Rebecca being reluctant to give up a child and described highly sensitive and personal events that, after checking out what I could through my research, appeared to coincide with Fanny's birth family sending her away to be adopted by relatives.

The things Rebecca told me about as well as the things my colleague interpreted on her own were not easily found through brief online reading, supposing either of them intended to falsify things for attention. Instances of discussing Fanny's adoption in public settings numbered so few that I could count them on one hand simply because I only have one recollection from that time and so little has been printed about it on a historical level. The odds of two people who did not know each other or talk to each other describing the same things or getting together to pull the wool over my eyes were extremely low. Still, I hesitated for a short time just because I couldn't fathom that it would be so easy for two souls who were separated in a past life to find each other again.

However, if souls need each other, nothing can stop one from finding the other. Some may discredit soul groups that partially come together through online activity but the universe is not antiquated. Just as soul groups remained intact through letters before modern conveniences, there is no reason why soul groups cannot utilize new ways to stay together as this world gets smaller and smaller with technology.

I meditated and prayed on the question of whether Rebecca was Fanny's birth mother in a past life or if we were being led into false hopes. I concentrated on asking for some sort of sign to clue me in on the truth or untruth of it. A few weeks later, the letter from Fanny's birth mother appeared in an online auction and not long after that, I was sent to a historical society in Connecticut that had possession of a painting of Fanny's maternal grandmother. Fanny's mother was one of only a few children who lived into adulthood.

I found that when a person follows a completely logical path, they can unintentionally miss information, guidance and support from the unseen universe. I stopped, I stepped back from the question and went quiet long enough for the universe to offer its own answers because there are simply going to be many times in life when a person cannot understand everything alone. Perhaps one of the lessons with Rebecca finding me and inadvertently sending me on the odyssey into Fanny's maternal family was that I needed to learn to trust things bigger than myself sometimes.

At the same time that I had possibly found a parent figure from a past life, another parent figure lay dying upstairs above me. Inside of the situation, I could not see the potential lesson in that, but looking back on it with clarity now; I believe I was shown proof that even if we lose people we love, they never really go away. The separation caused by life circumstances and death are only temporary. There will be another chance to make things right or complete lessons together, whether it happens between lives or in the next incarnation.

My stepfather lost his battle with cancer quietly at home on the evening of August 2, 2008. He endured suffering that I could not possibly imagine and even though it would take a while to be accustomed to life without his daily presence, the grieving process was not as devastating as it could have been. My family has relied on our faith that the death of a body is simply the passing of a phase. His body giving out did not mean he no longer existed. We knew he was watching over us with the rest of the soul group who was not incarnated at that time. I know my mother takes comfort in knowing that he is a spiritual presence in the way that Lawrence is a spiritual presence for me when it is needed. It certainly cuts deep to have to say goodbye but goodbye is not forever. Pain is temporary but love lasts forever.

CHAPTER NINETEEN

The obstacles in life can feel insurmountable when you are in the thick of them but then one day passes and then another day and a week and a month. Eventually, you allow yourself a minute to stop and look back, only to find that you made it through to the other side and you became a stronger person because of it. Challenges like quadriplegia, poverty, abuse or deaths of family members when added up together make my life sound as though it's been impossibly difficult to find any happiness. The truth of the matter is that had I not taken in the experiences from my past lives and learned from them, I would not have the tools to make the most of the life I live now.

The first year after my stepfather died was one of the most difficult in my life but I recognize that had one thing been altered in any way, I would not be where I am today. I may not have found strength in the ability of the soul group to hold a person up when times are difficult, whether people are aware that they all belong to soul groups or not. Many of the closest relationships I have now are a result of being open to the different facets of personal spirituality and the belief that there is a purpose for everything. We struggled financially, emotionally and mentally for months after he passed away and we still struggle in some ways but our bonds have strengthened because of the lessons he left us through his experience of cancer and passing. I know death is not the end. I know the body is merely a vehicle to take us through this world.

In the process of putting the pieces of Fanny together with myself, I put together smaller pieces of other past lives as well. Before I was reborn into Fanny's life, I passed through revolutionary France and met my end at the guillotine about a month after Queen Marie Antoinette was executed. I had gone through periodic bouts of nightmares through my life associated with riots while the royal family was under effective house arrest in the Tuileries Palace but I never had the fortitude to acknowledge it or look into it until I was well into adulthood.

My life in France was like a hyper-naïve version of my life in Maine, with an aristocratic background and a much more sheltered upbringing. I do believe there were subconscious shadows of the previous life in myself as Fanny by the way I tried to dress and decorate in a pseudo-opulent way much higher than the status of a minister's daughter or a professor's wife. Fanny named her last daughter Gertrude Loraine or Lorraine (I have seen both spellings) and Marie Antoinette, who I had loved like a goddess in France, had Lorraine in her formal name. I had been to the Palace of Versailles as a French noble and I attended a ball in the Palace of Versailles in the 1870s as Lawrence's wife. Lawrence himself was descended from Huguenots, and in revolutionary France, I had also been in love with another Huguenot, despite the social faux pas of it. My life in France ended violently and unfairly. I went to the guillotine a bitter, hurt, angry young woman and I believe some of those feelings carried over into being reborn into Fanny's life more than twenty-five years later, which left Fanny with lifelong bouts of depression and serious difficulty allowing herself to become close to people.

During the Elizabethan period, I had lived among nobility once more but it was not a pleasant life by any means. The things that carried over from that life involved an abusive husband and a historically mysterious death. I know what happened but since it is so debated, I choose not to comment on it typically. I have had such a paralyzing fear of staircases from that life that I freeze up, close my eyes and pray earnestly not to fall at the top of any staircase today. Falling, being pushed or throwing myself down the stairs, depending on which historian is consulted, is how I died on September 8, later to be Lawrence's birthday.

I encountered that Elizabethan husband from that life reincarnated today and went through a period of attraction much the way I had back then, but he has not grown or changed as a soul very much at all. The free will to exist in a state of learning or a state of stagnate ignorance is present for every soul. Encountering that man and getting my heart smashed again taught me that one of the hardest things we have to do as individual souls is recognize when others in our soul groups are not learning what they should. As much as it might cause emotional and spiritual trauma, it becomes necessary to let go of trying to help people who do not want to be helped. A person cannot be forced to learn from their mistakes. They have to choose to grow and move into new phases of their development. It was much harder in this case because he believed wholeheartedly in the truth of reincarnation and claimed to be spiritually enlightened, but nearly everyone soon recognized that he was stagnate in his growth and toxic to our own development. It is difficult to let go of people who should know better but some simply choose to live in the confines of dishonesty and manipulation.

People come and go out of our lives to varying degrees but what constitutes a successful, fulfilled life is being aware as much as one can about what can be learned from every encounter or experience. Positive or negative, each challenge, obstacle and situation has something to teach or affords an opportunity for a person to teach others. The success or failure of a life is determined by the free will of choosing to merely go through the motions of life or to soak in every possible experience and live with an appetite for life.

I began this journey as a toddler with no conscious understanding of the implications that my thoughts and memories would have as an adult. I never expected to be in a position today to be able to help people by sharing my memories of Fanny's life, but I know now that I would not change a moment of it. I spent a significant piece of my life trying to conform to society's expectations of what I should be, but in doing that, I suppressed the entire history of my soul and the fruits of the lessons just waiting to be picked. I almost missed out on becoming someone who considers more possibilities than those that are right under my nose. There is so much more to life than the tangible and the quest for more and more material possessions.

Sometimes people ask me if I still love Lawrence because of how vivid my memories are of him and the occasional presence of his spirit in my present life. I used to not know the precise way to answer that question because I am not living that life anymore, yet I am as protective of his legacy today as I was in supporting his choices then, even when I disagreed with them. There have been times, especially in the middle of the night when I'm alone with a book and a single lamp, when the hole in me that his absence in this life leaves feels as big as that of a widow's who has just lost her husband a few months ago.

Throughout history, however, there have been a myriad of stories about people whose love transcended time, who could not let go of it even after they died. Souls do not stop loving one another when a life ends. Mothers love their children and husbands love their wives no matter how much time passes, as evident by the stories of hauntings all over the world in which souls choose to stay rather than risk letting go of their loved ones.

It is not exclusive to romantic ghost stories. In my proverbial travels through the reincarnation community, I have encountered several other women like me who reincarnated but their soulmates or twin flames did not. One of them is the wife of an officer perhaps more famous than Lawrence but he was killed so abruptly in the Civil War that he never realized his death. I encountered another woman of a similar story except her partner was like Lawrence in that he died peacefully in old age. There is a sense of silent understanding when I meet people of that background. We don't have to explain things to each other because we have all lived it. We took the shape of a makeshift support group, checking in with one another from time to time, and confiding things that most of society refuses to understand.

I am a different person now. My hair is brown covered by red dye; my eyes are blue-gray, and my ethnicity being different than Fanny's does not make us look like striking twins as in the case of Jeffrey Keene and John B. Gordon. Very few cases are as striking as his but looking at Fanny gives the same sensation as looking at myself. Where Fanny was a singer and natural performer, I have serious anxiety about being watched by crowds despite my love of singing and music. Many of the facets of my character, habits and tastes have remained concurrent from life to life for centuries, but each new incarnation comes with individual circumstances to create choices, lessons and opportunities. Each life is connected to the others through the relationships created or destroyed, healed or wounded, and lessons we fail to conclude will be carried over into future lives until they are completed. The circumstances of life, society and the choices we make shape who we become, like an ever-changing piece of clay molded and shaped into something beautiful.

None of my lives have left a world-impacting legacy. I was never a musical prodigy like Mozart, or a wronged queen like Marie Antoinette, or a gilded young pharaoh like Tutankhamen. In the end of a life, wealth or power or possessions mean nothing. You cannot take a plasma television with you to the grave or into the next life. Nobody says, "I sure remember So-and-So's stuff," years, decades and centuries after a person passes away. My stepfather's last days were spent in a simple bed, in a simple room with no concern about what to do with the material things he acquired in his life. In a parallel light, when my life as Fanny came to an end, I laid in a bed without a concern for the things I had acquired and lost in that lifetime. From Lawrence's perspective, the only thing that concerned him was getting home fast enough to be there through the end but he did not make it in time.

A person can only take their deeds and the love they gave and received into the next life. Happiness is a choice. Allowing challenges to make you miserable and carrying around anger or hatred in your heart will only ingrain those negative things into your soul to be carried with you like an imprint overshadowing the happiness of lives ahead. The capacity to forgive and let go of negativity not only improves the chances of carrying that natural ability in the future, but it improves the quality of life at this moment. If I had not carried such anger and blackness through my last days in France, it is entirely possible that my existence in Fanny's life would have been just marginally easier.

In this life, I have been abused, neglected, forgotten and taken advantage of, but my journey through these past lives and seeing the snowball effect firsthand has taught me that holding onto negativity is only going to harm myself in the end. The incapacity to forgive, to let go and move on from trauma does not bring any revenge or harm upon those who hurt you. Hatred, toward yourself or other people, is simply a waste of energy that should be put toward better things. When you are wronged, all you can do is pick up the pieces, find the lesson in the experience and carry on with life.

Throughout the highs and lows of putting together the puzzle of this entire reincarnation process, the one theme that continues no matter what evidence I find is the continuance of love. It is the component that gives us all fuel for immortality. The very nature of the soul is energy and that by law of physics cannot be created or destroyed but changes form. I have found that love can never be destroyed even if the body dies away.

To say that I still love the person who was Joshua Lawrence Chamberlain at one time is true but "Lawrence" is only a small part of his soul. His soul is the literal other half to mine and if I love myself, then by definition, I love that soul as well. I am solidly aware of one other lifetime in which we were together and possibly three other incarnations. We switched genders in a much older lifetime and we lived in Africa, as far as I can tell from the flashes of memory. I was the husband, he was the wife and we were a completely different race, different language, culture, traditions, and so on, but the one thing that translated was love. That kind of unconditional understanding, love and peace comes through no matter what earthly circumstances change.

As with every other lifetime without him and every lifetime he lived without me, we go on and live perfectly happy, fulfilling existences. At the moment, I feel that I'm being taught the importance of independence and finding my own worth. Once a person learns to love and accept themselves, flaws and all, then the capacity to love others becomes limitless. I'm not quite there yet but I consider myself a work in progress, as everyone should also consider themselves. We all carry within us the capacity to unselfishly love if we find a way to let go of the blackness holding us back from fulfilling lives.

I know Lawrence is out there just like any of my other relatives who are no longer alive. I think about my past families every day, all the children I have given birth to, and the families and children I will have in the future. I have contributed to keeping my past home in Brunswick, Maine, restored and functioning, although I cannot contribute as much as I would like. I continue doing spiritual intuitive readings for people and teaching them that facing bad past events should be learned from rather than feared and avoided. The fear of not following the crowd in society needs to be eradicated because I see it holding people back from reaching their full potential every day. When I openly became myself and stopped hiding the fact that reincarnation is real, I felt free. I would like to live in a world where everyone else can taste that freedom too.

At the end of it all, when I sit in the quiet of Pine Grove Cemetery in Brunswick, Maine, asking myself if it's all worth it, I look at the row of graves under the ancient trees marking the Chamberlain phase of our past life history. The one thing that held our family together like so many other faceless families in the world was acceptance and love. Love gives us immortality.

ABOUT THE AUTHOR

Born in February 1982 to Lori and Curt Jones in Denver, Colorado, Jessica Jewett showed an early talent for all things creative. Despite her rare disability, Arthrogryposis, Jessica taught herself to write with her mouth before she entered kindergarten. Her first poem was completed in 1988 at the age of six, and she began her first illustrated short story in 1990, followed by the start of her first novel in 1994. She has worked in journalism, freelance writing and constantly evolves as a novelist. Her artwork has been exhibited in a gallery showing throughout the Southeast. She has numerous hobbies in artistic, paranormal and historical fields, which are often the subject of her writing. She resides in Atlanta, Georgia.

Made in the USA
Columbia, SC
16 August 2020